THE MAN WHO WOULD NOT DIE.

We Die Alone is the incredible story of a man who defied death and clung to life.

We Die Alone is a story no one would believe if the central figure, Jan Baalsrud, had not survived to prove it true, together with scores of witnesses who took part in his dramatic escape.

We Die Alone is a story of desperate violence, of warm friendship, charity, and sacrifice, and of one man's undying faith and triumphant spirit.

WE DIE ALONE

THE BANTAM WAR BOOK SERIES

This is a series of books about a world on fire.

These carefully chosen volumes cover the full dramatic sweep of World War II. Many are eyewitness accounts by the men who fought in this global conflict in which the future of the civilized world hung in balance. Fighter pilots, tank commanders and infantry commanders, among others, recount exploits of individual courage in the midst of the large-scale terrors of war. They present portraits of brave men and true stories of gallantry and cowardice in action, moving sagas of survival and tragedies of untimely death. Some of the stories are told from the enemy viewpoint to give the reader an immediate sense of the incredible life and death struggle of both sides of the battle.

Through these books we begin to discover what it was like to be there, a participant in an epic war for freedom.

Each of the books in the Bantam War Book series contains a dramatic color painting and illustrations specially commissioned for each title to give the reader a deeper understanding of the roles played by the men and machines of World War II.

WE DIE ALONE

David Howarth

BANTAM BOOKS · TORONTO · NEW YORK · LONDON

WE DIE ALONE

*A Bantam Book / published by arrangement with
Macmillan, Inc.*

PRINTING HISTORY
*Macmillan edition published November 1955
Book-of-the-Month Club edition published November 1955
Books Abridged edition published May 1956
Condensations appeared in Cavalier Magazine, June 1956
and Stag Magazine, August 1966
Bantam edition / September 1978*

Maps by Alan McKnight.
Drawings by Tom Beecham.

ISBN 0–553–12150–2

On mourra seul

PASCAL, 1623–1662

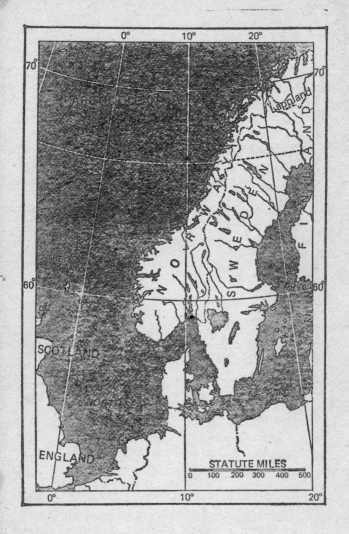

STATUTE MILES

0 100 200 300 400 500

Contents

Author's Note

I heard the bare bones of this story during the war, soon after it happened, and I mentioned it briefly in my book *The Shetland Bus*. All that I knew about it then was based on a report which was written in a Swedish hospital by a man called Jan Baalsrud. It was a graphic report, but Baalsrud was very ill when he wrote it, and it left a lot unsaid. One could see that there was much more in the story, some things which Baalsrud had forgotten and others he had never known, although he played the main part in it. But it was not until ten years later that I had a chance to talk it all over with him, and persuade him to come with me to the far north of Norway where it happened, to try to find out the whole truth of it.

Now that I have found it out and written it down, I am rather afraid of being accused of exaggeration. Parts of it are difficult to believe. But I have seen nearly all the places which are mentioned in this book, and met nearly all the people. Not one of the people knew the whole story, but each of them had a most vivid recollection of his own part in it. Each of their individual stories fitted together, and also confirmed what Baalsrud himself remembered. Some minor events are matters of deduction, but none of it is imaginary. Here and there I have altered a name or an unimportant detail to avoid offending people; but otherwise, I am convinced that this account is true.

WE DIE
ALONE

Jan Baalsrud

1

Landfall

Even at the end of March, on the Arctic coast of
northern Norway, there is no sign of spring. By then,
the polar winter night is over. At midwinter, it has
been dark all day; at midsummer, the sun will shine all
night; and in between, at the vernal equinox, the days
draw out so quickly that each one is noticeably longer
than the last. But the whole land is still covered thickly with ice and snow to the very edge of the sea.
There is nothing green at all: no flowers or grass, and
no buds on the stunted trees. Sometimes there are clear
days at that time of year, and then the coast glitters
with a blinding brilliance in the sunlight; but more
often it is swept by high winds and hidden by frozen
mist and driven snow.

It was on that coast, on the 29th of March, 1943,
that this story really began. On that day a fishing boat
made landfall there, six days out from the Shetland
Islands, with twelve men on board. Its arrival in those
distant enemy waters in the third year of the war,
within sight of a land which was occupied by the Germans, was the result of a lot of thought and careful
preparation; but within a day of its arrival all the plans
which had been made were blown to pieces, and everything which happened after that, the tragedies and adventures and self-sacrifice, and the single triumph,
was simply a matter of chance; not the outcome of any

1

plan at all, but only of luck, both good and bad, and
of courage and faithfulness.

That particular day was sunny, as it happened,
and the twelve men watched it dawn with intense excitement. It is always exciting to make the land after a
dangerous voyage; the more so when one's ship ap-
proaches the land at night, so that when daylight comes
a coast is revealed already close at hand. In that landfall there was an extra excitement for those men, because they were all Norwegians, and most of them were
about to see their homeland for the first time since
they had been driven out of it by the German invasion
nearly three years before. Above all, here was the supreme excitement of playing a dangerous game. Eight
of the twelve were the crew of the fishing boat. They
had sailed it safely across a thousand miles of the no-
man's-land of ocean, and had to sail it back when they
had landed their passengers and cargo. The other four
were soldiers trained in guerrilla warfare. Their journey
had two objectives, one general and one particular. In
general, they were to establish themselves ashore and
spend the summer training the local people in the arts
of sabotage; and in particular, in the following autumn
they were to attack a great German military airfield
called Bardufoss. In the hold of the boat, they had
eight tons of explosives, weapons, food and arctic
equipment, and three radio transmitters.

As the day dawned, they felt as a gambler might
feel if he had staked his whole fortune on a system he
believed in; except, of course, that they had staked
their lives, which makes a gamble even more exciting.
They believed that in a Norwegian fishing boat they
could bluff their way through the German coast defenses, and they believed that with their plans and
equipment they could live ashore on that barren land
in spite of the arctic weather and the German occupation; and on these beliefs their lives depended. If they
were wrong, nobody could protect them. They were
beyond the range of any help from England. So far, it
had all gone well; so far, there was no sign that the
Germans were suspicious. But the gleaming mountains

which they sighted to the southward, so beautiful and serene in the morning light, were full of menace. Among them the German coast watchers were posted, and soon, in the growing light, they would see the fishing boat, alone on the glittering sea. That morning would put the first of the theories to the test, and that night or the next would bring the boat and its crew to the climax of the journey: the secret landing.

At that time, in 1943, that remote and thinly populated coast had suddenly had worldwide importance thrust upon it. Normally, in time of peace, there is no more peaceful place than the far north of Norway. For two months every summer there is a tourist season, when foreigners come to see the mountains and the Lapps and the midnight sun; but for the other ten months of the year, the people who live there eke out a humble livelihood by fishing and working small farms along the water's edge. They are almost cut off from the world outside, by the sea in front of them and the Swedish frontier at their backs, and by bad weather and darkness, and by the vast distance they have to travel to reach the capital of their own country or any other center of civilization. They live a hard life, but a very placid one. They are not harassed by many of the worries which beset people in cities or in more populous countrysides. They take little account of time.

But when the Germans invaded Norway in 1940, the thousand miles of Atlantic seaboard which fell into their hands was the greatest strategical asset which they won; and when Russia entered the war, the far northernmost end of the coast became even more important, and even more valuable to Germany. The allied convoys to the Russian arctic ports, Archangel and Murmansk, had to pass through the narrow strip of open sea between the north of Norway and the arctic ice; and it was from north Norway that the Germans attacked them with success which had sometimes been overwhelming. Bardufoss was the base for their air attacks and their reconnaissance, and the coast itself provided a refuge for submarines and a safe passage from German harbors all the way to the Arctic Ocean.

As soon as the Germans had installed themselves on the northern coast, their position was impregnable. It was a thousand miles from the nearest allied base, and the country could not have been better for defense. A screen of islands twenty miles wide protects it from the sea, and among the islands are innumerable sounds through which defending forces could maneuver by sea in safety. The mainland itself is divided by a series of great fjords, with mountainous tongues of land between them. Beyond the heads of the fjords is a high plateau, uninhabited and mostly unsurveyed, snow-covered for nine months of the year; and across the plateau, marked by a cairn here and there among its deserted hills, is the frontier of Sweden, which was a neutral country then, entirely surrounded by others under German occupation. To attack the Germans in arctic Norway with any normal military force was quite impossible. Every island and every fjord could have become a fortress; and if the Germans had ever found themselves hard pressed in northern Norway, they could have reinforced their position by occupying Sweden, which would not have been to the advantage of the Allies.

In these circumstances, the voyage which had come to its end on that March morning had a possible importance out of all proportion to the size of the expedition. Great hopes of its outcome were held in London. Only four men were to be landed, but they were quite capable, with a little luck, of putting the air base at Bardufoss out of action long enough for a convoy to have a chance of getting through undetected; and the time was also ripe for the training of local people. The great majority of Norwegians up there would have gladly taken some positive action against the Germans, and would have done it long before if they had had any weapons and any instructions on how to set about it. Once the training was started, it would grow like a snowball.

The only reason why nothing of the kind had been done in Norway before was that it was so difficult to get there. Small parties of men on skis could get over the mountains across the border from Sweden, and a radio transmitter had been taken in that way and was installed in the town of Tromsö. But a saboteur's equipment was much too bulky and heavy to carry across the mountains, or to smuggle past the Swedes. The only way to take it was by sea.

By that time, a great many landings had been made in the southern part of Norway by fishing boats fitted with hidden armament, which sailed from a base in Shetland, and the resistance movement down there was well supplied and flourishing. But none of these boats, up till then, had tackled such a long and risky journey as the one to the north of Norway. The boat which had just accomplished it had come from the Shetland base. Its name was the *Brattholm*. It was 75 feet long, and had a single cylinder engine which gave it a speed of eight knots. Its appearance had been carefully preserved, so that it looked like any Norwegian fishing boat, and it had false registration numbers painted on its bows. But it was armed with seven machine guns hidden on mountings on deck, and each of its passengers had his own spare machine gun stowed somewhere where he could get it in a hurry.

The date when it sailed from Shetland, in the third week in March, had been a compromise which was not entirely satisfactory for anybody. The skipper and crew of the boat had to make up their minds between sailing in the depth of winter, when they would have the cover of the arctic night but would also have to weather the arctic storms, or in the late spring or early autumn, when the weather would probably be rather more moderate but the German defenses, and their air patrols in particular, would have the advantage of daylight. On the whole, from the skipper's point of view, it would have been better to go earlier than March, because his boat was sound and fit to stand up to any weather. But the passengers also had to be considered. If they had been landed in the worst of winter weather they might not have been able to keep themselves alive after they got ashore.

But still, the choice of March had been justified in

so far as the voyage had been a success. The weather had not been bad. The little boat had felt very conspicuous to the people on board it as it slowly steamed northward day after day, but it had only been sighted once, by a German aircraft about three hundred miles from land; and this aircraft, which was probably on a weather reconnaissance flight and not really concerned with stray fishing boats, had only circled around and then flown away.

So it seemed that whatever happened when they were sighted from the shore, at least the shore defenses could not have been warned about them, and would have no reason to guess that the humble boat they saw in front of them had crossed a thousand miles of the Atlantic. But it still remained to be seen whether the coast watchers would be deceived by *Brattholm*'s innocent appearance. It had worked often enough far-

Brattholm

ther south, but on a new bit of coast there was always the risk of infringing some local fishing regulation and so giving the game away. For all that the crew or the passengers knew, they might be pretending to fish in the middle of a minefield, or an artillery range, or some other kind of forbidden area, because nobody had been able to tell them before they left Shetland exactly where these kinds of defenses were.

At the tense moment of the dawn, all the four passengers were on deck. Wars often bring together people of very different character, and these four were as varied in experience and background as any four Norwegians could have been. Their leader was a man in his middle forties called Sigurd Eskeland. As a young man, he had emigrated to South America, and he had spent most of his adult life in the back of beyond in Argentina running a fur farm. On the day when he heard on the radio that Norway had been invaded, he got on his horse and left his farm in the hands of his partner, and rode to the nearest town to volunteer by cable for the air force. The air force turned him down on account of his age, but he worked his way to England and joined the army instead. He got into the Commandos, and then transferred to the Linge Company, which was the name of the military unit which trained agents and saboteurs for landing in occupied Norway. Long ago, before he went abroad, he had been a postal inspector in north Norway, so that he remembered something about the district he had been assigned to.

The other three men were very much younger. There was a radio operator called Salvesen, who was a member of a well-known shipping family. He had been a first mate in the Merchant Navy when Norway came into the war; but after a time that defensive job had begun to bore him, and when he heard of the Linge Company he volunteered to join it as an agent.

The other two were specialists in small arms and explosives, and they were close friends who had been through a lot of queer experiences together. Both of them were 26 years old. One was called Per Blindheim. He was the son of a master baker in Ålesund on the west coast of Norway, and in his youth he had served his time on the bread round. Superficially, he was a gay and very handsome young man in the Viking tradition, tall and fair and blue-eyed; but hidden beneath his boyish appearance and behavior, he had a most compelling sense of justice. When the Russians attacked Finland, it seemed to him so wrong that he threw up his job and left home to join the Finnish army. When the World War began and his own country was invaded, he hurried back and fought against the Germans; and when the battle for Norway was lost, he set off for England to begin it all over again, escaping from the Germans by way of Russia, the country against which he had fought a few months before.

The other one of this pair of friends, and the fourth of the landing party, was Jan Baalsrud. To look at, Jan was a contrast to Per; he had dark hair and gray-blue eyes, and was of a smaller build altogether. But he had the same youthful quality, combined with the same hidden serious turn of mind; a depth of feeling which neither of those two would show to strangers, but one which all four of the men must have needed to carry them through the hardships of their training and bring them to where they were.

Jan had been apprenticed to his father, who was an instrument maker in Oslo, and had only just started his career when the invasion came. He had fought in the army, and escaped to Sweden when there was no chance to fight anymore. By then he had discovered a taste for adventure, and he volunteered as a courier between Stockholm and Oslo, and began to travel to and fro between neutral Sweden and occupied Norway, in the service of the escape organization which the Norwegians had founded. Luckily for him, he was caught and arrested by the Swedes before he was caught by the Germans. They sentenced him to five months' imprisonment, but after he had served three months of his sentence he was let out and given a fortnight to leave the country.

This was easier ordered than done; but he got a Russian visa and flew to Moscow, where he landed inauspiciously among Russian celebrations of German victories. However, the Russians treated him well and sent him down to Odessa on the Black Sea; and it was while he was waiting there for a ship that he first met

Per Blindheim, who was on the same errand. The two traveled together to England by way of Bulgaria, Egypt, Aden, Bombay, South Africa, America and Newfoundland. When they got to London, the first of the sights that they went to see was Piccadilly Circus; and while they were standing looking rather glumly at this symbol of their journey's end, and wondering what was going to happen next, Jan saw in the crowd an English officer he had known in Stockholm. This man recruited them both forthwith for the Linge Company, and there they found a job which fulfilled all their hopes of adventure.

These, then, were the four men who stood on the deck that March morning at the climax of a year of preparation. They had trained together in the highlands of Scotland, doing forced marches of thirty and forty miles with packs across the mountains, living out in the snow, studying weapons and underground organization, doing their quota of parachute jumps, and learning to draw and cock an automatic and score six hits on a half-man-sized target at five yards, all in the space of three seconds; finally learning all the vulnerable points of airfields; and incidentally, enjoying themselves tremendously. They were tough and healthy, and elated at the imminence of danger; and very confident of being able to look after themselves, whatever the dawn might bring.

2

The Fight in Toftefjord

On that sort of expedition it was useless to make a detailed plan, because nobody could foresee exactly what was going to happen. The leader always had a degree of responsibility which few people are called upon to carry in a war. The orders he was given were in very general terms, and in carrying them out he had nobody whatever to advise him. His success, and his own life and the lives of his party, were in his own hands alone.

As leader of this party in north Norway, Eskeland had a specially heavy load to carry. From the south, or from any country from which a lot of refugees had escaped to England, a fund of information had been collected about German dispositions and the characters and politics of innumerable people, and the information was always being renewed. The leader of an expedition could be told, in more or less detail, whom he could trust and whom he should avoid, and where he was most likely to meet enemy sentries or patrols. But information about north Norway was scanty. A good many people had escaped from there, but the only route they could follow was across the mountains into Sweden, where they were interned. Many of them were content to stay in internment and wait for better times; and even those who made the effort to escape again, and managed to pass on what they knew to the British intelligence services, had usually been held by the Swedes for a matter of months, so that all that they could tell was out of date. Eskeland had been given the names of a few people who were known to be sound, but beyond that very little could be done to help him. Once he left Britain, he could only depend on his own training and wit and skill.

He had been as thorough as he possibly could be in his preparations. Ever since he had known he was to lead a landing from a fishing boat, he had pondered in a quiet way over every emergency he could foresee. On the high seas, the skipper of the boat was in command, and out there the problems had been comparatively simple. The boat might have been overcome by stress of weather, which was a matter of seamanship; or its one single-cylinder engine might have broken down, which was a job for the engineers; or it might have been attacked by aircraft, which would have been fought with the boat's own "Q-ship" armament. But now that it had closed the coast, he had to take charge, and now anything might happen and an instantaneous decision might be needed. For the present, the boat's first line of defense was for its guns to be kept hidden, so that it seemed to be innocently fishing. But once they got into the constricted waters of the sounds among the islands, they might meet a larger ship with heavier armament at short range at any moment, and then the boat's armament would be nothing but a hindrance. They might still bluff their way out as a fishing boat, but they could not hope to fight an action at two or three hundred yards. Apart from anything else, a single shot in their cargo might blow them all to pieces. The only way they could prepare for that kind of encounter, as Eskeland foresaw it, was to hide every vestige of warlike equipment and to lure the enemy ship to within pistol shot. Then, by surprise, there was a chance of boarding it and wiping out its crew.

During the past night, as *Brattholm* approached the coast, Eskeland and his three men had begun to

prepare for this possible crisis. They had cleaned and
loaded their short-range weapons, Sten guns and car-
bines and pistols; and they had primed hand grenades
and stowed them in convenient places, in the wheelhouse and galley, and along the inside of the bulwarks,
where they could be thrown without warning on board
a ship alongside. In case it came to close quarters, he
and his three men had all put on naval uniforms although they were soldiers, so that the Germans would
not be able to identify them as a landing party.

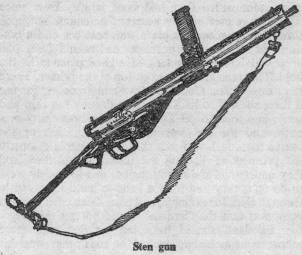

Sten gun

But even while they made these preparations, they
all knew that although with luck they might be success-
ful in that sort of hand-to-hand action, they had very
little chance of getting away with their lives. Between
themselves and safety there were the thousand miles of
sea which they had crossed. They might hope to kill or
capture the entire crew of even a larger ship; but unless
they could do it so quickly that no radio signal could
be sent, and unless it happened in such a remote place
that nobody heard the gunshots, all the German defenses would be alerted; and then, it was obvious,

Brattholm at eight knots would not get very far. The only hope of escape then, and it was a small one, was to scuttle the ship and get ashore.

Eskeland had provided for this too. The three radio transmitters in their cargo were a new type still graded top secret, and they also had a few important papers: ciphers, maps, and notes about trustworthy people and German defenses. They all understood quite clearly that they had to defend these things with their lives. It went without saying. It was one of the basic rules which they had been taught. Ever since they had entered enemy waters, the papers had been stowed in an accessible place with matches and a bottle of petrol; and a primer, detonators and fuses had been laid in the eight tons of high explosives in the hold. The transmitters were on top of the primer. There were three fuses. One had a five-minute delay, for use if there seemed to be a chance to destroy the ship and cargo and then to get away. The next was thirty seconds, and the last was instantaneous. Each of the twelve men on board was able to contemplate soberly the prospect of lighting the instantaneous fuse, and they understood the circumstances in which they were to do it; if they had tried a hand-to-hand fight with a German ship, for example, and been defeated. The main point was that the Germans should not get the cargo.

Eskeland should have felt satisfied with these preparations as he approached the coast; they were intelligently conceived, and carefully carried out. But on that very day a change of plan was forced upon him, and he was reminded, if there had been any doubt about it, how sketchy his information was. They had intended to land on an island called Senja, about forty miles southwest of the town of Tromsö; but as they approached it, steaming peacefully through the fishing zone, they sighted a trawler coming out toward them. They altered course to the eastward, waiting to see what was going to happen. The trawler reached the open sea at the outer edge of the islands, and then it turned back on its track and went into the sounds again. As it turned, they saw a gun on its foredeck. It was a patrol ship, where no patrol ship had been reported.

At that stage of the expedition, it was their job to avoid trouble rather than look for it, and there was no sense in trying to land their cargo on the one island, from all the hundreds in the district, which they now knew for certain was patrolled. Their disguise had worked so far. They had been seen, and passed as a fishing boat. The sensible thing to do was to choose another island; and after a discussion, they agreed upon one a little farther north. It is called Ribbenesöy. It is due north of Tromsö, thirty miles from the town. On the chart of it, they found a little bay on the northeast side which seemed to offer good shelter, and one of the men who had been in that district before remembered the bay as a remote and deserted spot. At about midday on the 29th of March, they set course toward it. Its name is Toftefjord.

It was late in the afternoon by the time they reached the skerries which lie scattered in the sea for seven miles off the shore of Ribbenesöy, and began to pick their way among them. In bad weather the passage which they used is impassable. There are thousands of rocks awash on either side, and the whole area becomes a mass of spray in which no marks are visible. But on that day the sea was calm and the air was clear. They sighted the stone cairns which are built as seamarks on some of the biggest rocks, and passed through into sheltered water. They steamed below a minute island called Fuglö, which rises sheer on every side to a black crag a thousand feet high; they skirted the north shore of Ribbenesöy, a steep, smooth, gleaming sheet of snow which sweeps upward to the curved ice-cornice of a hill called Helvedestind, which means Hell's Peak; and as the light began to fade they crept slowly into Toftefjord, and let go an anchor into clear ice-blue water.

When the engine stopped, Toftefjord seemed absolutely silent. After six days of the racket and vibration of a Norwegian fishing boat under way, the mere absence of noise was unfamiliar; but there is always a specially noticeable silence in sheltered places when the

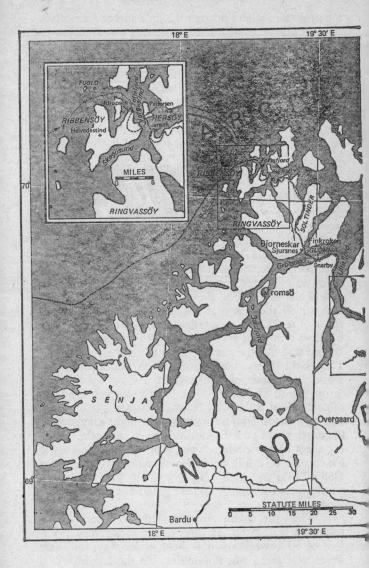

18° E
19° 30' E

FUGLO

Idrupsen
Pedersen
RIBBENSÖY
HERSÖ
Helvedestind
Jansen

Skardosund

MILES
0   5

RINGVASSÖY

70°

Toftefjord

RIBBENSÖY

RINGVASSÖY

SOLTINDER

Bjorneskar
Finkroken
Sjursnes
GLOMMA
Grötsund
Snarby
Ullsfjord

Skerring

Tromsö

Balsfjord

S E N J A

Overgaard

N O R

69°

STATUTE MILES
0   5   10   15   20   25   30

Bardu

18° E
19° 30' E

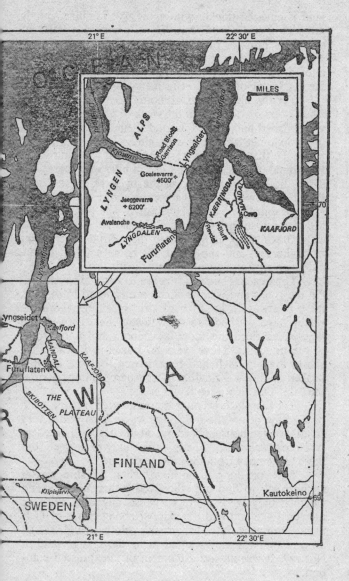

land is covered thickly with snow. All familiar sounds
are muted and unresonant. There are no footfalls, no
sounds of birds or running water, no hum of insects or
rustle of animals or leaves. Even one's own voice seems
altered. Even without reason, in places hushed by snow,
the deadening of sound seems menacing.

Yet the appearance of Toftefjord was reassuring.
They stood on deck when the work of coming to anchor
was finished and looked around them, talking involun-
tarily in quiet voices. It was almost a perfect hiding
place. To the south and west and east it was shut in by
low rounded hills. The tops of the hills were bare; but
in the hollows by the shore, the twigs of stunted arctic birch showed black against the snow. To the north
was the entrance of the bay, but it was blocked by a
little island, so that one could not see into it from outside. *Brattholm* was quite safe there from observation
from the sea, and she could not be seen from the air
unless an aircraft flew almost overhead.

The beaches showed that the bay was always calm.
On the rocks and islands which are exposed to the sea,
there is always a broad bare strip of shore where the
waves have washed the snow away; but there in the
landlocked fjord the snow lay smooth and thick down
to the tidemark. There were no tracks in it. Close inshore, the sea itself had been frozen, but the ice had
broken up and was floating in transparent lumps around
the ship. The air was cold and crisp.

Yet the place was not quite deserted. At the head
of the bay, below the hill, there was a barn and a very
small wooden house. Close by, on the beach, there were
racks for drying fish. There was nobody to be seen, but
there was smoke from the cottage chimney.

The first thing to be done, when the ship was at
anchor, was to find out who lived in that cottage, and
whether they were likely to cause any difficulties or
danger. Eskeland and the skipper changed out of their
naval uniforms into fishermen's clothes and rowed
ashore. Perhaps they wanted to be the first to land in
Norway. It was always a moment of unexpressed emotion.

They soon came back, saying there was nothing to worry about. There was a middle-aged woman with her two children, a boy of about sixteen and a girl who was younger. Her husband was away at the cod fishing in the Lofoten islands, and she did not expect him back for several weeks. Eskeland had told her that they had stopped to make some engine repairs. There was no reason why she should be suspicious, and there was no telephone in the house. It would be quite easy to keep an eye on her and the children. She had told him, incidentally, that no Germans had ever been in Toftefjord. In fact, she herself had never seen a German. Her husband had had to hand in his radio set to the authorities, and her nearest neighbors were two miles away. She was quite out of touch with the world and with the war.

The landing party and the crew had dinner in relays, leaving a watch on deck. They were very cheerful. For one thing, it was the first good dinner they had had on board, not only because it is difficult to do much cooking in a fishing boat at sea, but also because the cook had been seasick and Jan Baalsrud, who had deputized for him, had had rather limited ideas. The landing party were happy also because the voyage was successfully ended, and they could really get to work. For soldiers, a sea voyage is always tedious; they are usually pleased to get out of the hands of sailors.

While they ate, they discussed the coming night. When the four men of the sabotage group had started to prepare themselves for the expedition, they had divided among them the enormous territory they were to cover, and each of them had studied his own part of it in detail. But by changing the landing place from Senja, they had put themselves farther north than any of the districts they knew best. However, Eskeland remembered a little about Ribbenesöy from his days as a postal inspector, and he had taken the precaution of learning the names of a few reliable people in the neighborhood. One of these was a merchant who kept a small general store on the south side of the island. Eskeland had never met him, but his name was on a list in

London of men who could be trusted. His shop was
only a few miles away, and they decided to make a start
that night by going to see him and asking him about
hiding their cargo. Experience in the southern part of
Norway had shown that shopkeepers were often more
adept than anyone else at providing a temporary hiding
place for stores. Most shops had outhouses and back
premises which in wartime were nearly empty. Cases of
weapons had often been stacked among cases of gro-
ceries. A shopkeeper was also a likely man to tell them
where they could get a local boat to take them into
Tromsö, where they would find their principal "contacts."

So Eskeland set off, as soon as it was dark, in
Brattholm's motor dinghy. He took the ship's engineer
with him to look after the motor, and another man who
had been added to the crew as an extra hand because
he knew the district. They steered out of the bay and
followed the shore of Ribbenesöy to the eastward,
through the sound which separates it from the next island of Hersöy, and then back, close inshore along the
south side of the island. They saw the shop and a few
buildings near it, and a wooden jetty, silhouetted against
the afterglow in the western sky. There was a light in
the shop, and another on board a boat which was lying,
with its engine running, a few yards off the end of the
jetty.

As they approached the jetty, they passed close
to the boat. It was a small fishing craft with two or three
men on board. It would have seemed strange to pass
it without a word, and besides, a small local fishing craft
was one of the things they wanted. So they hailed it
and told the men the story they had prepared: that they
had engine trouble and wanted a lift to Tromsö to get
some spare parts.

The men were sympathetic, and only mildly in-
quisitive, as fishermen would naturally be. They talked
all around the subject, in the infinitely leisurely manner
of people who live on islands. They asked what make
of engine it was, and what horsepower, and what spare

parts were needed. They recommended a dealer in
Tromsö, and suggested ringing him up in the morning
and getting him to send the parts out in the mailboat,
which would probably be as quick as going to fetch
them, and certainly cheaper. They asked what the herring fishing was like, and where the *Brattholm* was
bound for.

Everyone who lives under false pretences gets
used to receiving perfectly useless advice with patience
and cunning. Eskeland and the engineer, in this un-
realistic conversation across the dark water, answered
the questions carefully one by one, until a chance came
for them to put the one question in which they were interested.

"I suppose you couldn't take us into Tromsö?"

This started a long explanation of how they were
waiting there for a man to bring them some bait which
they had paid for already, so that they could not afford
to miss him, and they said all over again that they
could not see any sense in going all the way to Tromsö
for spares when there was a telephone up in the shop.
But they told Eskeland that if he was really set on
wasting money by going there, the shopkeeper had a
boat and might take him in.

Eskeland thanked them and left them, understanding perhaps that to a man who lives in the outer islands
Tromsö is a very distant city, and a journey there is not
a thing to be undertaken lightly. At least, he had
learned that the shop at the head of the jetty was really
the one he wanted.

The shopkeeper was in bed when they got to the
house; but when they knocked he came downstairs in
his underclothes and took them into the kitchen. They
apologized for coming so late, and told the same story
again. But with him, they only told it as a means of
introduction, to make conversation till he felt at ease
with them and they could tell him the true reason for
their visit. While they were talking, they slipped in
questions about the Germans. No, he said when they
asked him, the Germans had really been no trouble out

there on the islands. They had never been ashore. He
saw their convoys passing in the channel south of Ribbenesöy, and they had been out laying minefields. And
of course they sent out notices which had to be stuck
up everywhere: "Contact with the enemy is punished by
death." There was one downstairs in the shop. He had
heard stories about how they behaved in Tromsö, but as
for himself, he had never had anything to do with
them.

Carefully feeling his way, Eskeland began to
broach the subject of his cargo, and his need to go to
Tromsö. The shopkeeper was willing to take one or
two men to town in his boat. Eskeland offered to pay
him a substantial sum of money for his help. It was the
size of this sum which first impressed on the shopkeeper
that he was being asked to do more than hire out a
boat. He looked puzzled; and then, because it would
be unjust to involve a man in what they were doing
without giving him an idea of the risks he was running,
and because the man had such an excellent reputation,
Eskeland told him that they had come from England.

At this, his expression changed. At first he was
incredulous. One of them gave him a cigarette, and he
took it and lit it; and the English tobacco seemed to
convince him that what they said was true. Then, to
their surprise, they saw that he was frightened.

He began to make excuses. He couldn't leave the
shop. It wasn't fair to leave his wife alone in the house
these days. There were the animals to attend to. Fuel
for the boat was difficult to come by.

Slowly and reluctantly, they had to admit to themselves that it was useless to try to persuade him. An
unwilling nervous helper would be a danger and a
liability. Yet they could not understand how a man who
had been so highly recommended could be so cowardly
in practice. The vast majority of Norwegians, as everybody knew, would have been delighted by a chance to
do something against the Germans. They puzzled over
his behavior, and told him they were disappointed in
him.

"But why did you come to me?" he asked plaintively. "What made you think I'd do a thing like that?"

They told him they had heard he was a patriot; and then the truth came out, too late, and they saw the mistake which they had made. The man told them he had only been running the shop for a few months. Its previous owner had died. His name was the same, so there had been no need to change the name of the business.

There was nothing left to do then except to impress on him as clearly as they could that he must never tell anyone what they had told him. He promised this willingly, glad to see that they had accepted his refusal. In his relief, he even recommended two other men who he thought would give them the help they needed. Their names were Jenberg Kristiansen and Sedolf Andreasson. They were both fishermen, and they lived on the north shore of the island, beyond Toftefjord. He felt sure they would be willing.

Eskeland and his two companions left him then, with a final warning that he must never mention what he had heard that night.

They went back to their dinghy, annoyed and slightly uneasy. There was no reason to think that the shopkeeper was hostile, or that he would do anything active to harm them. Not one man in a thousand would go out of his way to help the Germans. But many Norwegians of the simpler sort were prone to gossip, and any man whose own safety was not at stake was potentially the nucleus of a rumor. It was a pity, but the risk, so far as they could see, was small, and without entirely recasting their own plans there was nothing much they could do about it. It was sheer bad luck that the one man they had selected from the lists in London should have died, and even worse luck that another man with the same name should have taken his house and business. But it could not be helped. At least, he had given them new contacts.

They set off back toward Toftefjord, to tell the

rest of the party what had happened. On the way, they were overtaken by the fishing boat which had been lying off the jetty of the shop. Its crew had got their bait and were on their way to the fishing grounds. They took the dinghy in tow; but just before they came to the mouth of Toftefjord the skipper shouted that they had forgotten a rope, some part of their fishing gear, and that they had to go back to the shop to fetch it. He cast the dinghy off. Eskeland went on into Toftefjord, and saw the fishing boat turn around and steam away.

What happened when the skipper and crew of the fishing boat got back to the shop will never exactly be known. The shopkeeper had gone back to bed, but they called him out again, and this time his wife joined them to hear what was going on. He said he was feeling sick and giddy. He thought it was due to the cigarettes the strangers had given him. His brother was one of the crew, and he and the skipper plied him with questions about the strange boat and the three unknown men. Before very long, the shopkeeper had told them everything.

It was probably during this conversation that a new and appalling fear struck him. Was it possible that the three men were German agents sent to test him? He had heard people say that the Germans sent men about in the islands, dressed in civilian clothes, to do that very thing: to say that they came from England, and then to report anyone who offered to help them. What was more likely than that they should pick on him, a merchant, a man with a certain standing in the community, and one who had only recently set up in business? He was thankful, now he came to think of it, that he had refused to help them. And yet, had he been careful enough? He racked his brains to remember exactly what he had said about Germans. He felt sure he had been indiscreet. There had been something about minefields. That was probably secret. Of course, he said to the others, the only way to make sure of his position, the only safe thing to do, was to report what the men had told him. Supposing they were German agents, it would not be enough only to have refused to help them. They would be waiting now to see if he reported them. If he didn't, they would get him anyhow.

The three men discussed this dilemma for an hour. The shopkeeper's wife listened in distress at his agitation. His brother was in favor of doing nothing. It would be a bad business, he admitted, if the men were Germans; but on the other hand, if he reported them and it turned out that they had really come from England, it would be far worse. The trouble was, it was impossible to be sure; but on the whole, he thought it was right to take the chance.

With this decision, after a long confusing argument, the skipper and the shopkeeper's brother left for the fishing again. The shopkeeper himself went back to bed, still feeling sick and dizzy. He could not sleep. He knew what it meant to be disloyal to the Germans, or rather, to be caught at it: the concentration camp for himself and perhaps for his wife as well; the end of the little business he had begun to build up; the end of everything. He lay there imagining it all. But to make sure of his safety was so easy. There was the telephone downstairs in the shop. And yet, if they were really Norwegians, and had really come from England, and the neighbors got to know he had told the Germans, he knew very well what they would say, and he knew what his customers would do. Those men had sounded like Norwegians: not local men, but they spoke Norwegian perfectly. But of course there might be Norwegian Nazis, for all he knew, who would do a job like that for the Germans. And was it possible to come in a fishing boat in March all the way from England? That sounded an unlikely story. Perhaps the best thing would be to get up and go over to Toftefjord and speak to them again and see if they could prove it. But then the Germans were too clever to do anything by halves; they would have their proofs all ready. How could he tell? How could he possibly find out?

The shopkeeper lay all night, sick with fear and confusion. Toward the morning, the last of his courage ebbed away. About seven, he crept down to the shop, and picked up the telephone. He had thought of a compromise. He asked for a man he knew who had an official post in the Department of Justice.

In Toftefjord, when Eskeland had told the others about the two merchants with the same name, they agreed that there was nothing to be done. The man had promised not to talk, and short of murder they could not think of any way of making more sure of him than that. So Eskeland set off again, not very much discouraged, to see the two fishermen the shopkeeper had recommended.

This time he got the answer he expected. There was no point in telling these men the story about spare parts. By then, it was about three o'clock in the morning, and even in the Arctic, where nobody takes much notice of the time of day, people would not expect to be woken up at such an hour with any ordinary request. He did not ask them to go to Tromsö either. Most of the first night was already gone, and the most urgent need was to get the cargo ashore so that *Brattholm* could sail again for Shetland.

The two fishermen agreed at once, enthusiastically, to hide it in some caves which they knew. Eskeland did not tell them the whole story. He did not mention England, but left them with the impression that he had brought the cargo from the south of Norway, and that it contained food and equipment for the home forces to use when the tide began to turn. But the two men did not want to be told any more about it. If it was anti-German, that seemed to be good enough for them. They said they would come to Toftefjord at half-past four on the following afternoon to pilot *Brattholm* out to their hiding place, so that everything would be ready for unloading as soon as it was dark.

It was daylight by the time the dinghy got back to Toftefjord. Eskeland and the men who were with him were tired, not merely by being out all night, but by the long hours of careful conversation. When they came aboard, they found that Jan Baalsrud, the only one of the landing party who had not been either to the shop or the fishermen, had been at work all night checking over their small arms again. As an instrument maker, Jan loved the mechanisms of guns and always took particular care of them; and like Eskeland, he had been a little worried about the shopkeeper.

They made breakfast, and talked about the shop again. It was only two hours' steaming from Tromsö, somebody pointed out, for any kind of warship; so if they had really had the bad luck to hit upon a Nazi and he had reported them, they would surely have been attacked by then. Dawn would have been the obvious time for the Germans to choose. But dawn was past, and Toftefjord was as quiet and peaceful as before. They agreed in the end that the landing party should stay on watch till ten o'clock. If nothing had happened by then, it really would look as if that particular danger was over; and then the landing party would turn in and leave some of the crew on watch till the fishermen came at half-past four.

The morning passed. The only thing which was at all unusual was the number of aircraft they could hear. There was the sound of machine-gun fire too, from time to time. It was all out at sea. But none of the air craft flew over Toftefjord. It sounded as though there was a practice target somewhere beyond the islands, and that seemed a possible explanation. The air forces at Bardufoss must have somewhere for training, and the sea or the outer skerries would be a likely place. As the day went by, the men began to relax. By noon, they were reassured. Eskeland and his party went below to sleep, leaving half of the crew on deck.

A shout awoke them: "Germans! Germans!" They rushed for the hatch. The men on watch stood there appalled. Two hundred yards away, coming slowly into the fjord, there was a German warship. As the last of the men reached the deck, it opened fire. At once they knew that the aircraft were on patrol stopping the exits from the sounds. There was no escape for *Brattholm*. Eskeland shouted "Abandon ship! Abandon ship!"

That was the only order. They knew what to do. Somebody ran up the naval flag to the mizen head. The crew leaped down into one of the boats and cast off and rowed for shore. The German ship stopped and lowered two boats. Troops piled into them and made for the shore a little farther north. Jan Baalsrud and Salvesen poured petrol on the cipher books and set them all on fire, and cast off the second dinghy and held it ready in the lee of the ship out of sight of the Germans. Eskeland and Blindheim tore off the hatch covers and climbed down among the cargo and lit the five-minute fuse.

With her boats away the German ship began to approach again. It was firing with machine guns and a three-pounder, but the shots were going overhead. The Germans meant to capture them alive: they were not expecting much resistance. Eskeland called from the hold, "Jan, hold them off!" Jan took a sub-machine gun and emptied the magazine at the German's bridge. The ship stopped for a moment, and then came on again. Eskeland jumped up from the hold, calling to the others "It's burning," and all of them climbed down into the dinghy, and waited. They knew the drill: to wait till the last possible minute hidden in *Brattholm*'s lee before they started to try to row away.

Eskeland sat looking at his wristwatch, with his arm held steadily in front of him. One of the others held on to the side of *Brattholm*'s hull. Two were ready at oars. One minute had gone already. They could not see the German ship from there. They could hear it approaching the other side of *Brattholm*, firing in bursts at *Brattholm* and at the crew in the other dinghy. Per Blindheim said, "Well, we've had a good time for twenty-six years, Jan." Eskeland said, "Two minutes." Jan could see the crew. They had got to the shore. Two were still in the dinghy with their hands up. Three were on the beach. One was lying in the edge of the water. One was trying to climb the rocks, and machine-gun bullets were chipping the stones above him and ricocheting across the fjord. Eskeland said, "Three minutes." The German landing party came into sight, running along the shore toward the place where the crew had landed, jumping from rock to rock. When they got near, the firing stopped, and for a few seconds there was no sound but the shouts of German orders. "Three and a half," Eskeland said. "Cast off."

They began to row, keeping *Brattholm* between them and the Germans. In that direction, toward the head of the fjord, it was two hundred yards to shore. But the German ship was very close, and it was much bigger than *Brattholm*. Before they had gone fifty yards they were sighted, and at this point-blank range the Germans opened fire. The dinghy was shot full of holes and began to sink. But the German ship was slowly drawing alongside *Brattholm,* and the last quarter of a minute of the fuse was burning down, and the fascination of watching the trap being sprung blinded them to the miracle that so far they had not been wounded.

The ship and *Brattholm* touched, and at that very moment the explosion came. But it was nothing, only a fraction of what it should have been. Only the primer exploded. The hatch covers were blown off and the front of the wheelhouse was wrecked, but the German ship was undamaged. There were shouts and confusion on deck and for a few seconds the firing stopped. The ship went full speed astern. *Brattholm* was burning fiercely. In that momentary respite, the men in the dinghy rowed for their lives, but the ship swung around till its three-pounder came to bear. Its first shot missed the dinghy. And then the whole cargo exploded. *Brattholm* vanished, in the crack of the shock wave, the long roar in the hills, the mushroom of smoke streaked with debris and blazing petrol. Eskeland was blown overboard. Jan leaned out and got him under the arms and hauled him on to the gunwale, and the German gunner recovered and a shot from the three-pounder smashed the dinghy to pieces. They were all in the water, swimming. There were seventy yards to go. The Germans brought all their guns to bear on the heads in the water. The men swam on, through water foaming with bullets, thrusting the ice aside with their heads and hands.

All of them reached the shore. Jan Baalsrud stumbled through the shallows with his friend Per Blindheim beside him. As they reached the water's edge Per was hit in the head and fell forward half out of the water. With a last effort, Jan climbed a rocky bank and found cover behind a stone. As he climbed he had been aware that his leader Eskeland had fallen on the beach and that Salvesen, either wounded or exhausted, had sunk down there unable to make the climb. He shouted to them all to follow him, but there was no answer. A bullet hit the stone above his head and whined across the fjord. He was under fire from both sides. He looked behind him, and saw the Germans who had landed. Four of them had worked around the shore and crossed the hillside fifty yards above him to cut off his retreat. He was surrounded.

At the head of the fjord there is a little mound, covered with small birch trees. Behind it the hills rise steeply for about two hundred feet. A shallow gully divides them. Within the gulley the snow lies deeply, a smooth steep slope only broken by two large boulders. The patrol came floundering down the hill, pausing to kneel in the snow and snipe at Jan with rifles. Caught between them and the fire from the ship he could find no cover. But to reach him the patrol had to cross the little dip behind the mound, and there for a moment they were out of sight. He got up and ran toward them. He could not tell whether they would come over the mound, through the birches, or skirt around it to the left. He crept around it to the right. He had been wearing rubber seaboots, but had lost one of them when he was swimming, and one of his feet was bare. He heard the soldiers crashing through the brittle bushes. Soon, as he and the patrol each circled around the mound, he came upon their tracks and crossed them. It could only be seconds before they came to his. But now the foot of the gully was near, and he broke cover and ran toward it.

They saw him at once, and they were even closer than before. An officer called for him to halt. He struggled up the first part of the gully, through the soft sliding snow. The officer fired at him with a revolver and missed, and he got to cover behind the first boulder in the gully and drew his automatic.

Looking back down the snow slope, he watched the officer climbing up toward him with three soldiers following close behind. The officer was in Gestapo uniform. They came on with confidence, and Jan remembered that so far he had not fired a shot, so that they possibly did not know that he was armed. He waited, not to waste his fire. Beyond the four figures close below him, he was aware of uproar and confusion, shouting and stray shots in the fjord. As he climbed, the officer called to Jan to surrender. He was out of breath. Jan fixed on a spot in the snow six yards below him. When they reached there, he would shoot.

The officer reached it first. Jan squeezed the trigger. The pistol clicked. It was full of ice. Twice more he tried, but it would not work, and the men were within three paces. He ejected two cartridges, and it fired. He shot the Gestapo officer twice and he fell dead in the snow and his body rolled down the slope over and over toward the feet of his men. Jan fired again and the next man went down, wounded. The last two turned and ran, sliding down the snow to find cover. Jan jumped to his feet and began the long climb up the gully.

For a little while, it was strangely quiet. He was hidden from the fjord by one side of the gully. The snow was soft and deep and difficult, and he often slipped with his rubber boot. With all his strength, he could only climb slowly.

Above the second boulder, for the last hundred

feet, the gully opened out into a wide snow slope, perfectly clean and white and smooth, and as soon as he set foot on it he came into sight of the German ship behind him.

In his dark naval uniform against the gleaming snow up there he was exposed as a perfect target for every gun on the warship and the rifles of the soldiers on the beaches. He struggled in desperation with the powdery snow, climbing a yard and slipping back,

clawing frantically with his hands at the yielding surface which offered no hold. The virgin slope was torn
to chaos by the storm of bullets from behind him.
Three-pounder shells exploding in it blew clouds of
snow powder in the air. He could feel with sickening
expectation the thud and the searing pain in his back
which would be the end of it all. The impulse to hide,
to seek any refuge from this horror, was overwhelming.
But there was nowhere to hide, no help, no escape
from the dreadful thing that was happening to him. He
could only go on and on and on, choking as his lungs
filled with ice crystals, sobbing with weariness and rage
and self-pity, kicking steps which crumbled away beneath him, climbing and falling, exhausting the last of
his strength against the soft deep cushion of the snow.

He got to the top. There were rocks again, hard
windswept snow, the crest of the hill, and shelter just
beyond it. He dropped in his tracks, and for the first
time he dared to look behind him. The firing died.
There below him he could see the whole panorama
of the fjord. Smoke hung above it in the sky. The German ship was at the spot where *Brattholm* had been anchored. On the far shore, a knot of soldiers were
gathered around the crew. Nearer, where he had
landed, his companions were lying on the beach, not
moving, and he thought they were all dead. All around
the fjord there were parties of Germans, some staring
toward him at the spot where he had reached the ridge
and disappeared, and others beginning to move in his
direction. In his own tracks before his eyes the snow
was red, and that brought him to full awareness of a
pain in his foot, and he looked at it. His only injury
was almost ludicrous. It was his right foot, the bare
one, and half his big toe had been shot away. It was
not bleeding much, because the foot was frozen. He
got up and turned his back on Toftefjord and began to
try to run. It was not much more than ten minutes
since he had been sleeping in the cabin with his
friends, and now he was alone.

3

Hunted

If Jan had stopped to think, everything would have seemed hopeless. He was alone, in uniform, on a small bare island, hunted by about fifty Germans. He left a deep track, as he waded through the snow, which anyone could follow. He was wet through and had one bare foot, which was wounded, and it was freezing hard. The island was separated from the mainland by two sounds, each several miles wide, which were patrolled by the enemy, and all his money and papers had been blown up in the boat.

But when a man's mind is numbed by sudden disaster, he acts less by reason than by reflex. In military affairs, it is at moments like those that training is most important. The crew's training had been nautical, the sea was their element, and when their ship disappeared before their eyes and they were cast ashore without time to recover themselves and begin to think, their reaction was to lose hope and to surrender. But Jan had been trained to regard that barren hostile country as a place where he could live and work for years. He had expected to go ashore and to live off the land, and so, when the crisis came, he turned without any conscious reason to the land as a refuge, and began to fight his way out. If his companions had not been wounded or overcome by the icy water, no doubt they would have done the same thing, although none of them knew then, as they learned later, that any risks and any sufferings were better than surrender.

For the moment, his thoughts did not extend beyond the next few minutes. He thought no more than a hunted fox with a baying pack behind it, and he acted with the instinctive cunning of a fox. It served him better, in that primitive situation, than the complicated processes of reason. On the southern slopes of the island there was less snow. Here and there, where the rocks were steep, he found bare patches, and he hobbled toward them and crossed them, leaving no track, laying false trails, doubling back on the way he had come, jumping from stone to stone to leave the snow untrodden in between. But there was no cover. Wherever he went, he could be seen from one part of the island or another; and as the shock of the battle faded and his heart and lungs began to recover from the effort of his climb, he began to believe that although he had escaped, it could only be minutes before the Germans ran him down.

Running blindly here and there among the hills, hampered by his wounded foot, he had no idea how far he had come from Toftefjord, and before he expected it he found himself facing the sea again. Below him on the shore there were some houses and a jetty, and from Eskeland's description he recognized the shop. He had crossed the island already. He remembered that the shopkeeper had a boat, and he thought of trying to steal it. But the water in front of him was wide and clear, and the Germans would be over the hill behind him at any moment. He knew he could not get out of sight in a boat before they came.

He went on, down to the shore a little way from the jetty. There at least was a narrow strip of beach which was free of snow, and he could walk along it, slowly and painfully, without leaving any tracks at all. He turned to the left, away from the shop, back toward Toftefjord. He felt intolerably lonely.

There were two little haysheds by the shore. He wanted to creep into one and hide there and burrow in the hay and get warm and go to sleep. They were obvious hiding places. But even as he began to think of it, he knew they were too obvious. They were isolated. He pictured himself hidden there in the dark, hearing the Germans coming along the beach, and their expectant shouts when they saw the sheds, and himself trapped in there while they surrounded him. The very uselessness of the haysheds impressed upon him that there really was no hiding place for him on that dreadful island. If he stayed on the island, wherever he hid he would be found.

As he scrambled along the beach he was coming nearer, though he did not know it, to the sound which Eskeland and the others had passed through on their way to the shop. It is called Vargesund, and it is full of rocks, in contrast to the wide open waters to the north and south. The largest of the rocks is about half an acre in extent. As soon as Jan saw this little island, he knew what he had to do, and for the first time he saw a gleam of hope. He hurried to the edge of the water, and waded in, and began to swim again.

It was only fifty yards to the rock, and in spite of his clothes and his pistol and his one seaboot, he had no difficulty in swimming across. But when he dragged himself out of the mixture of ice and water, and climbed over to the far side of the rock, the effect of this second swim began to tell on him. He had to begin to reckon with the prospect of freezing to death.

There was a minute patch of peat on top of the islet, and someone had been cutting it. He got down below the peat-bank and started to do exercises, keeping an eye on the hills of the main island. His bare foot was quite numb, although running had made an unpleasant mess of the raw end of his toe. He took off his seaboot and moved his one sock from his left foot to his right. It seemed a good idea to have a boot on one foot and a sock on the other. He stamped his feet, crouching down below the bank, to start the circulation and try to ward off frostbite.

It was only a very short time before the Germans came in sight, and for the next two hours he watched them, at first with apprehension, and then with a grow-

ing sense of his own advantage. They came slowly, in
straggling line abreast, pausing to challenge every
stone, with a medley of shouts and orders and counter-
orders; and Jan, watching them critically in the light of
his own field training, remembered one of the many
things he had been told and had only half believed:
that the garrisons of that remote part of Norway were
low-grade troops whose morale was softened by isolation and long inactivity. Gradually, as he watched
their fumbling search, he began to despise them, and
to recognize beneath that formidable uniform the signs
of fallibility and even fear. They were probably clerks
and cooks and batmen, dragged out unwillingly at a
moment's notice from comfortable headquarters billets
in the town. He could guess very well what they would
think of having to hunt a desperate armed bandit
among ice and rocks and snow.

It was dusk when the first party of them came
along the beach, but he could see them clearly because
they were using torches which they flashed into dark
crevices. They passed his island without a glance behind them out to sea. So far, it seemed not to have
crossed their minds that he might have swum away.

When it was dark, the confusion increased. They
were scattered in small groups all over the hills. Each
group was signaling to others with its torches. Men
were shouting their own names, afraid that their
friends would mistake them for the bandit. Now and
then a single shot echoed from hill to hill. That could
only mean that nervous men were firing at fancied
movements in the dark. Slowly it dawned on Jan, with
a feeling of intense elation which gave him new
strength and courage, that for all their numbers, they
were afraid of him.

That opportunity to study the German army at its
worst was worth months of military training, because
after it he never again had the slightest doubt that he
could outwit them till the end.

At the same time, he was becoming more aware
of the dangers of his natural surroundings. A human
enemy, however relentless and malevolent he may be,

has human weaknesses; but nobody can trifle with the Arctic. In immediate terms, Jan knew that if he stayed where he was in his wet clothes, he would be dead before the morning.

Of course, there was only one alternative: to swim again. He could swim back to Ribbenesöy, among the Germans, or he might conceivably swim across the sound, to Hersöy, the next island to the eastward. One way or the other, he had to find a house where he could go in and get dry and warm. He had only seen two houses on Ribbenesöy, the shopkeeper's and the one in Toftefjord, and both of them were out of the question. He knew from the chart that there were others farther west, but by that time they were probably full of Germans. Across the sound, on Hersöy, he had seen a single lonely house, but he had no idea who lived there.

He looked at Vargesund, and wondered if it was possible. In fact, it is 220 yards across, but it was difficult for him to guess its width in the darkness. The far shore was only a shadow between the shining water and the shining hills. The surface of the sound was broken here and there by eddies: the tide had begun to set. In health and strength he could easily swim the distance; but he could not judge the effects of the tide and the cold and his own exhaustion. He stood for a long time before he made up his mind. He did not want to die either way, but to drown seemed better than to freeze. He took a last look behind him at the flashing torches of the soldiers, and stumbled down the rocks and waded in and launched himself into the sea again.

It is a mercy that the ultimate extremes of physical distress often get blurred in memory. Jan hardly remembered anything of that third and longest swim, excepting an agony of cramp, and excepting the dreadful belief that he was just about to die; an experience most people encounter once or twice in a lifetime, but one he had had to face so many times on that single day. It was after he had given up any conscious struggle, and admitted his defeat, and was ready to welcome his release from pain, that some chance eddy swept

him ashore on the farther side and rolled his limp body
among the stones, and left him lying there on his face,
groaning and twisted with cramp, and not able to move
or to think of moving.

Seconds or minutes later, in the mists of half-
consciousness, there were voices. There were footsteps
on the beach, and the clink of stones turning. He wondered with a mild curiosity whether the words he
could hear were German or Norwegian, and from
somewhere outside himself he looked down with pity
on the man who lay beaten on the shore and the people who approached him; because if they were German, the man was too weak to get away. But slowly his
dim enfeebled brain began to accept a fact which was
unforseen and strange on that day of death and violence.
They were children's voices. There were children, coming along the beach and chattering in Norwegian. And
suddenly they stopped, and he knew they had seen
him.

He lifted his head, and there they were, two little
girls, holding hands, wide-eyed with horror, too frightened to run away. He smiled and said, "Hullo. You
needn't be afraid." He managed to turn around and sit
up. "I've had an accident," he said. "I do wish you
could help me." They did not answer, but he saw
them relax a little, and he realized that when they had
seen him, they had thought that he was dead.

Jan loved children; he had looked after his own
young brother and sister after his mother died. Perhaps
nothing in the world could have given him strength of
mind just then, except compassion: the urgent need to
soothe the children's fear and make up for the shock
which he had given them. He talked to them calmly.
His own self-pity and despair had gone. He showed
them how wet he was, and made a joke of it, and they
came nearer as their fright gave way to interest and
wonder. He asked them their names. They were Dina
and Olaug. After a while he asked if their home was
near, and whether they would take him there, and at
the idea of bringing him home and showing their par-

ents what they had discovered they brightened up and helped him to his feet. The house was not far away.

Two women were there, and the rest of their children. They exclaimed in horrified amazement at the frozen, limping, wild disheveled man whom the little girls led in. But the moment he spoke to them in Norwegian their horror changed to motherly concern and they hurried him into the kitchen, and took him to the fire and brought him towels and put the kettle on.

Of all the series of acts of shining charity which attended Jan in the months which were to come, the help which these two women gave him on the first night of his journey was most noble, because they knew what had happened just across the sound, and they knew that at any moment, certainly by the morning, the Germans would be pounding on their door. They knew that their own lives and the lives of all their children would hang on a chance word when they came to face their questioning. Yet they opened their door at once to the stranger in such desperate distress, and cared for him and saved his life and sent him on his way, with no thought or hope of any reward except the knowledge that, whatever price they paid, they had done their Christian duty. Their names are Fru Pedersen and Fru Idrupsen.

The first thing Jan did was to warn them all that the Germans were after him, and that when they were questioned they must say that he came in carrying a pistol and demanded their help by force. He brought out his pistol to emphasize what he said. As soon as he had made quite sure that they understood this, and that even the children had a clear idea of what they should do and say, he sent two of them out as sentries, and told them to warn him at once if they saw a boat coming into the sound.

Fru Idrupsen, it turned out, was the woman from Toftefjord. She had run to the hills with her children when the shooting started, and she had seen most of what happened from the top of the island. She had rowed across the sound to take refuge with her neigh-

bors. Fru Pedersen had a grown-up son and daughter
and two young children. Her son was out fishing, but
she expected him back at any minute. Her husband,
like Fru Idrupsen's, was away for the Lofoten fishing
season and would not be home till it ended.

All the time Jan was talking, the two women were
busy with the practical help which he needed so badly.
They gave him food and a hot drink, and helped him
to take off his sodden clothes. They found him new dry
underclothes and socks and a seaboot Herr Pedersen
had left behind, and they hung up his uniform to dry,
and rubbed his feet and legs till the feeling began to
come back to them, and bandaged the stump of his
wounded toe.

Twice while they worked to revive him, the sentries came running in to say that a boat was coming.
Each time Jan pulled on his steaming jacket and trousers and the seaboots, one his own and one Herr Pedersen's, and gathered together everything which belonged
to him and ran out of the house and up into the hills.
But each time the boat passed by.

Between these alarms, he rested and relaxed. That
humble Norwegian kitchen, with the children gathered
around him speaking his native tongue, was more
homely than any place he had seen in the three years
he had been abroad. The warmth, and the sense of
homecoming, and the contrast of family life after the
fearful tension of the day, made him drowsy. It was
difficult to remember that outside in the darkness there
still were ruthless men who would shoot him on sight,
and wreck that home if they found him there, and
carry the children off to captivity and the mothers to
unmentionable torment. Such violence had the quality
of a dream. And when he dragged his mind back to
grapple with reality, Jan found himself faced with a
doubt which often came back to him later: ought he
to let such people help him? Was his own life worth it?
Was he right as a soldier, to let women and children
put their lives in such terrible danger? To save them
from the consequence of their own goodness, ought he
not go out, and fight his own battle alone? But for the

moment, these questions went unanswered, because he was not fit to make any such decision. Fru Pedersen and Fru Idrupsen had taken him in hand, and they treated him as an extra child.

When he had been there half an hour or so, the eldest son of the Pedersen family came home. He had heard the explosion in Toftefjord, but did not know what had happened. They told him the story, and as soon as he had heard it he took it as a matter of course that a wounded survivor should be sitting in his mother's kitchen while the Germans scoured the islands round about. As his father was not at home, it was up to him to get Jan away to safety. He began to debate the question of how to do it.

The first thing was to rest. For one thing, there was no knowing when Jan might get another chance, and for another it would be madness to go out in a boat while the Germans were still there. And after that, the boy said, when he had rested, he ought to get away from the islands altogether, to the mainland. Any island, however big it was, might be a trap, not only because you might find your retreat cut off, but also because everyone on an island knew everyone else's business. If he stayed another day in Hersöy, everyone would know he was there. But on the mainland, if they did come after you, you could always go on a stage farther; and gossip did not spread there quite so fast. Altogether, he would be safer there. Besides, that was the way to Sweden.

This was the first time Jan had paused to think of an ultimate escape. Up till then, it had only been a matter of dodging for the next few hours, and he had still thought of north Norway as his destination. That was where he had set out for, and he had arrived; and although he had lost his companions and all his equipment, he had not admitted to himself that the whole expedition was a failure. He still hoped to do part of his job there, at least, as soon as he had got his strength back and shaken off the Germans. But the people who lived there, as he now began to see, all thought at once of Sweden for a man in such serious trouble. It was a

difficult journey, but not a very long one; about eighty
miles, in a straight line; if you could travel in straight
lines.

The trouble was, the boy went on, he only had a
rowboat himself, and they could never row to the
mainland. Just south of them was the sound called
Skagösund, which was two miles wide. On the other
side of that was Ringvassöy, an island about twenty
miles square, and south of that again you had to cross
Grötsund itself, which was the main channel into
Tromsö from the north and was four miles wide and
full of patrol boats. The best he could do himself was
to row Jan across to Ringvassöy before the morning.
But he knew a man there called Jensen who was all
right, and he had a motorboat and was meaning to go
into Tromsö some day soon. His wife was the midwife
over there, and he had a permit and was always moving about with his boat. He could easily put Jan ashore
on the mainland.

Jan listened gratefully as this plan unfolded. He
was glad for the moment to have everything thought
out for him, and was ready to fall in with any idea
which would take him away from Toftefjord.

When it was all decided, and he was resting, the
eldest son of the Toftefjord family went out in his boat
to see what had happened at his home, and to find out
for Jan if there was any sign of the rest of his party. He
was away for a couple of hours. When he came back,
Jan knew for certain that of all the twelve men, he was
the only one who was not either killed or captured.
Toftefjord itself was quiet. There were still parties of
Germans searching the distant hills. The slopes of the
fjord were littered with scraps of planking. The boy
had found the remains of a gasoline barrel, and seen
an ammunition belt hanging in a tree. But there was no
one, alive or dead, on the beaches. The German ship
had left. It was steaming slowly up the north side of the
island, using a searchlight. Jan's friends, or their
bodies, must have been taken aboard it. Eskeland and
Per Blindheim and all the others were gone, and he

could never expect to see them again. There was nothing he could do except to go on alone.

He left the house on Hersöy very early in the morning, well before it was light. Fru Pedersen and Fru Idrupsen watched him go and brushed aside his thanks, which could certainly not have been adequate for what they had done. The boy took him down to his boat and they got aboard and pushed her off into the sound. Jan felt fit again and ready for anything. They turned to the southward and began to row, past the place where he had landed from his swim, past the shop, and then out across the open water, heading for Ringvassöy, with Toftefjord astern. Everything was peaceful.

4

Seaboots in the Snow

In moments of calm, Jan often thought about his family, as all soldiers of all armies think in war. So far as he knew, they were still in Oslo: his father, and his young brother Nils, and his sister. His sister's name was Julie, but none of them ever called her that because they thought it was old-fashioned; they had always gone on calling her Bitten, which was the nickname he had invented for her when he was eight and she was a baby. When his mother died, he had been sixteen, Nils ten, and Bitten only eight; and so he had suddenly had to be very much more grown up than he really was; he had had to take care of the children when his father was at work, and even shop and cook and wash for them for a time till his aunt could come to the rescue.

They had always been a closely united family, both before and after that disaster, until the morning just after the invasion when his orders had come and he had left home on an hour's notice. But somehow a special affection had grown up through the years between himself and Bitten. Young Nils was a boy and an independent spirit who had always been able to stand on his own feet; but Bitten had turned to him more and more for advice, and he had become very fond of her, and proud of her, and deeply interested in her growing-up.

Perhaps this big brotherly affection had been the deepest emotion in Jan's life, when fortune landed him in Toftefjord when he was twenty-six. At any rate, leaving Bitten had hurt more than anything when the time came. He had tried to make the break as quick and painless as it could be when he knew he had to do it. He had waited around that morning till he knew she would be coming home from school, and he had met her in the street on his way to the station just to tell her he was going. She was fifteen then, and he had never seen her since. For the first few months, while he was in Norway and Sweden, he had been able to write to her sometimes, using a false name so that if the letters got into the wrong hands she would not get into trouble for having a brother who was still opposing the Germans after the capitulation. In his letters he had begged her to stay on at high school, not to be in a hurry to get a job; but he had never known if she had taken that advice. While he was in prison in Sweden he had a few letters from her, sending him press cuttings about netball games she had played in. It had made him smile to think that she wanted him to be interested in netball when he was just beginning a prison sentence; but it had also made him very homesick. Since he had left Sweden and started his journey to England, he had never heard of her at all. That was nearly three years ago. She would be eighteen now: grown up, he supposed. He sorely wished that he knew if she was happy.

Sitting in the boat that early morning, as the boy from Hersöy rowed him across the sound, Jan had every reason to think of his family. It had always been on his mind since he started to train as an agent that he would have to be careful to protect them from reprisals if anything went wrong. Now that capture and death were so close to him, he had to remind himself of the one and only way he could protect them: to refuse to be captured, and to die, if he had to die, anonymously. He had nothing on him to identify him or his body as Jan Baalsrud, and that was as it should

be: if worst came to worst, the Germans would throw
him into a grave without a name. His father and Nils
and Bitten would never know what had happened to
him. He would have liked them to know he had done
his best; but to leave them in ignorance was the price of
their safety.

Something the boy said brought this forcibly to
his mind. The boy meant to take him to Jensen's house
and introduce him and make sure that he was safe;
but Jan had to ask him to put him ashore out of sight
of the house and leave him. He explained the first
principle of any illegal plan: that nobody should know
more than he needs. It was a pity that the boy and his
family knew Jan was going to Jensen, but there was no
need for Jensen to know where he came from. You
might trust a man like your brother, he said, but it was
no kindness to burden him with unnecessary secrets,
because no man alive could be certain he would not
talk if he was caught and questioned. What your
tongue said when your brain was paralyzed by drugs
or torture was not a mere matter of courage; it was
unpredictable, and beyond any self-control. Jan himself would be the only one who knew everyone who
helped him; but he had his pistol, and he solemnly
promised this boy, as he promised more people later,
that he would not let them catch him alive. So the two
of them parted on the shore of Ringvassöy, and the
boy backed his boat off and turned away into the darkness, leaving Jan alone.

Jan owned nothing in the world just then except
the clothes he was wearing, and a handkerchief and a
knife and some bits of rubbish in his pockets, and his
pistol. He had navy blue trousers and a sweater and
Herr Pedersen's underclothes, and a Norwegian naval
jacket, a warm double-breasted one with brass buttons
and a seaman's badges, though he had never been a
seaman, and was not even very sure if he could row.
The jacket had the Norwegian flag sewn on its shoulders, with the word NORWAY in English above it. He
had lost his hat. He was amused at the odd footprints

which his two rubber boots left in the snow, one
English and one Norwegian. There was something
symbolic there, if you cared about symbols.

There were a dozen houses in that part of Ringvassöy, but he easily picked out Jensen's. The lights
were on, and there were voices inside. He hoped that
might mean that Jensen was making an early start on
his trip to Tromsö. He went to the back door, and hesitated a moment, and knocked. A woman opened the
door at once, and he asked if Jensen was at home. No,
she said, he had left for Tromsö the morning before,
and would not be back for two or three days.

At this disappointing news Jan paused for a moment uncertainly, because he did not want to show
himself to people who could not help him. He would
have liked to make an excuse and go away; but he saw
surprise and alarm in her face as she noticed his uniform in the light of the lamp from the doorway.

"I'm in a bit of trouble with the Germans," he
said. "Have you got people in the house?"

"Why, of course," she said. "I have my patients.
But they're upstairs. You'd better come inside."

That explained the lights and the voices so early
in the morning. He had not made allowances for
what a midwife's life involves. He went in, and began
to tell her a little of what had happened, and what he
wanted, and of the danger of helping him.

Fru Jensen was not in the least deterred by danger. She had heard the explosion in Toftefjord, and already rumors had sprung up in Ringvassöy. The only
question she asked was who had sent Jan to her house,
and when he refused to tell her and explained the reason why, she saw the point at once. She said he was
welcome to stay. She was very sorry her husband was
away, and she herself could not leave the house at
present, even for a moment. But there was plenty of
room, and they were used to people coming and going.
He could stay till the evening, or wait till Jensen came
home if he liked. He would be glad to take him to the
mainland. But she could not be sure how long he

would be away, and perhaps it would be risky to try to ring him up in Tromsö and tell him to hurry back.

"But you must be hungry," she said. "Just excuse me a moment, and then I'll make your breakfast." And she hurried upstairs to attend to a woman in labor.

Jan felt sure he would be as safe in her hands as anyone's. He could even imagine her dealing firmly and capably with Germans who wanted to search her house. If you were trying to think of a hiding place, there could hardly be anywhere better than a labor ward, because even the Germans might hesitate to search there. And yet it would be so impossibly shameful to use it. It might fail; it might not deter the Germans. Jan had all a young bachelor's awe and ignorance of childbirth; but he had a clear enough vision of German soldiers storming through that house, and himself forced to fight them there, and failing perhaps, and having to blow out his brains. If it came to that, he was ready to face it himself; one always knew it might happen, one could think of it calmly. But to involve a woman in something like that at the very moment of the birth of her baby, or perhaps to see a newborn infant shot or trampled underfoot—that was too appallingly incongruous; it could not bear to be thought about at all.

Besides this, there was another practical, strategic consideration. He was still much too close to Toftefjord. If the Germans really wanted to get him, it would not take them long to turn Ribbenesöy inside out: they had probably finished that already. And the obvious place for them to look, when they were sure he had left the island, was where he was now, on the shore of Ringvassöy which faced it. Their search would gradually widen, like a ripple on a pond, until they admitted they had lost him; and until then, at all costs, he must travel faster than the ripple.

When Fru Jensen came back and began to lay the table, he told her he had decided to move on. She did not express any feeling about it, except to repeat that he was welcome to stay if he wanted to; if not, she would give him some food to take with him. She began to tell him about useful and dangerous people all over her island. There were several ways he could go: either by sea, if he happened to find a boat, or along either shore of the island, or up a valley which divides it in the middle. But if he went up the valley, she warned him, he would have to be careful. People in those remote and isolated places were inclined to take their politics from the clergyman or the justice of the peace, or the chairman of the local council, or some other such leader in their own community; they had too little knowledge of the outside world to form opinions of their own. In the valley there happened to be one man who was a Nazi, or so she had heard; and she was afraid a lot of people might have come under his influence. If a stranger was seen there, he was certain to hear of it; and although she could not be sure, she thought he might tell the police. Of course, most of Ringvassöy, she said, was quite all right. He could go into almost any house and be sure of a welcome. And she told him the names of a lot of people who she knew would be happy to help him.

It was still early when Jan left the midwife, fortified by a good breakfast and by her friendliness and fearless commonsense. He wanted to get away from the houses before too many people were about; but it was daylight, and it was more than likely someone would see him from a window. It was a good opportunity to be misleading. He started along the shore toward the west. In that direction, he might have gone up the valley or followed the coastline around the west side of the island. But when he was out of sight of the last of the houses, he changed his direction and struck off into the hills, and made a detour behind the houses to reach the shore again farther east. He had made his plans now a little way ahead. The next lap was to walk thirty miles to the south end of the island.

It looked simple. He remembered it pretty clearly from the map, and during his training it would have been an easy day. He knew that maps of mountains

are often misleading, because even the best of them
do not show whether a hill can be climbed or not; but
he was not prepared for quite such a misleading map
as the one of that part of Norway. In the normal
course of events, nobody ever walks far in the northern
islands. The natural route from one place to another
is by sea. The sea charts are therefore perfect; but the
most detailed land map which existed then was on a
scale of about a quarter of an inch to a mile, and it
made Ringvassöy look green and smoothly rounded.
No heights were marked on it. There were contours,
but they had a vague appearance, as if there had been
more hope than science in their drawing. One might
have deduced something from the facts that the only
houses shown were clustered along the shores, and that
there was no sign of a single road; but nothing on the
map suggested one tenth of the difficulty of walking
across the island in the winter.

Jan had arrived there in the dark, and if he had
ever seen the island at all, it was only in that momentary glimpse when he had come over the hill from
Toftefjord with the Germans close behind him. So he
set off full of optimism in his rubber boots; but it took
him four days to cover the thirty miles.

He was never in any immediate danger during
that walk. The only dangers were the sort that a com-
petent mountaineer can overcome. Once he had disappeared into the trackless interior of the island he was
perfectly safe from the Germans until he emerged
again. But it was an exasperating journey. It had new
discomfort and frustration in every mile, and the most
annoying things about it were the boots. Jan was a
good skier; like most Norwegians, he had been used to
skiing ever since he could walk: and to cross Ringvassöy on skis might have been a pleasure. Certainly
it would have been quick and easy. But of course his
skis had been blown to pieces like everything else; and
there can hardly be anything less suitable for deep
snow than rubber boots.

He had started with the idea of following the
shore, where the snow would be shallower and harder

and he would have the alternative of going along the beach below the tidemark. But on the very first morning he found it was not so easy as it looked. He soon came to a place where a ridge ran out and ended in a cliff. He tried the beach below the cliff, but it got narrower and narrower until he scrambled around a rock and saw that the cliff face ahead of him fell sheer into the sea. He had to go back a mile and climb the ridge. It was not very steep, but it gave him a hint of what he had undertaken. The wet rubber slipped at every step. Sometimes, where the snow was hard, the climb would have been simple if he could have kicked steps; but the boots were soft, and to kick with his right foot was too painful for his toe. He had to creep up slowly, one foot foremost, like a child going upstairs. But when the snow was soft and he sank in it up to his middle, the boots got full of it, and came off, and he had to grovel and scrape with his hands to find them.

At the top of the ridge, when he paused to take his breath, he could see far ahead along the coastline to the eastward; and there was ridge after ridge, each like the one he was on, and each ending in a cliff too steep to climb.

He started to go down the other side, and even that was painful and tedious. Down slopes which would have been a glorious run on skis, he plodded slowly, stubbing his toe against the end of the boot, and sometimes falling when the pain of it made him wince and lose his balance.

But still, all these things were no more than annoyances, and it would have been absurd to have felt annoyed, whatever happened, so long as he was free. He felt it would have been disloyal, too. He thought a lot about his friends as he floundered on, especially of Per and Eskeland. He missed them terribly. Of course he had been trained to look after himself, and make up his own mind what to do. In theory he could stand on his own feet and was not dependent on a leader to make decisions for him. But that was not the same thing as suddenly losing Eskeland, whom he admired tremendously and had always regarded as a bit wiser and more capable than himself, someone he could always rely on for good advice and understanding. And still less, in a way, did his training take the place of Per, who had shared everything with him for so long. Jan knew his job, but all the same it was awful not to have anyone to talk it over with. As for what was happening to his friends, he could not bear to think about it. He would have welcomed more suffering to bring himself nearer to them in spirit.

In this mood, he forced himself on to make marches of great duration: 24 hours, 13 hours, 28 hours without a rest. But the distances he covered were very short, because he so often found himself faced with impassable rocks and had to go back on his tracks, and because of the weather.

The weather changed from one moment to another. When the nights were clear, the aurora glimmered and danced in the sky above the sea. By day in sunshine, the sea was blue and the sky had a milky radiance, and the gleaming peaks of other islands seemed light and insubstantial and unearthly. The sun was warm, and the glitter of snow and water hurt his eyes, though the shadows of the hills were dark and cold. Then suddenly the skyline to his right would lose its clarity as a flurry of snow came over it, and in a minute or two the light faded and the warmth was gone and the sea below went gray. Gusts of wind came whipping down the slopes, and clouds streamed across the summits; and then snow began to fall, and frozen mist came down, in gray columns which eddied in the squalls and stung his face and hands and soaked him through, and blotted out the sea and sky so that the world which he could see contracted to a few feet of whirling whiteness in which his own body and his own tracks were the only things of substance.

In the daytime, he kept going in these storms, not so much for the sake of making progress as to keep himself warm; but when they struck him at night, there

was no question of keeping a sense of direction, and
one night he turned back to take shelter in a cowshed
which he had passed four hours before.

He stopped at two houses along the north shore
of the island, and was taken in and allowed to sleep;
and oddly enough it was the wounded toe that served
him as a passport to people's help and trust. Rumors
had gone before him all the way. It was being said
that the Germans had started a new search of every
house, looking for radio sets, which nobody was allowed to own. Everyone had already guessed that this
search had something to do with what they had heard
about Toftefjord, and as soon as they learned that
Jan was a fugitive, they jumped to the conclusion that
the Germans were searching for him. And indeed, if
the search was a fact and not only a rumor, they were
probably right. This made some of them nervous at
first. Like the shopkeeper, they were frightened of
agents provocateurs, and Jan's uniform did not reassure
them; it was only to be expected that a German agent
would be dressed for his part. But the toe was different.
The Germans were thorough, but their agents would
not go so far as to shoot off their toes. When he took
off his boot and his sock and showed them his toe, it
convinced them; and he slept soundly between his
marches, protected by men who set faithful watches to
warn him if Germans were coming.

Always they asked who had sent him to them,
and some of them were suspicious when he would not
tell them. But he insisted, because he was haunted by
the thought of leaving a traceable series of links which
the Germans might "roll up" if they found even one of
the people who helped him. Such things had happened
before, and men on the run had left trails of disaster
behind them. To prevent that was only a matter of
care. He never told anyone where he had come from,
and when he asked people to recommend others for
later stages of his journey, he made sure that they gave
him a number of names, and did not tell them which
one he had chosen. Thus nobody could ever tell, be-

cause nobody knew, where he had come from or
where he was going.

The last stretch of the journey was the longest.
Everyone he had met had mentioned the name of
Einar Sörensen, who ran the telephone exchange at a
place called Bjorneskar on the south side of the island.
All of them knew him, as everybody knows the telephone operator in a country district, and they all spoke
of him with respect. Bjorneskar is opposite the mainland, and if anyone could get Jan out of the island,
Einar Sörensen seemed the most likely man. But if he
refused, on the other hand, or if he was not at home, it
would be more than awkward, because the south end
of the island was infested with Germans, in coastal bat-
teries and searchlight positions and patrol boat bases,
defending the entrance to Tromsö. Bjorneskar was a
kind of cul-de-sac. The shore on each side of it was
well populated and defended, and Jan could only reach
it by striking inland and going over the mountains. It
would be a long walk, and there was no house or
shelter of any kind that way; if there was no help when
he got to the other end, it was very unlikely that he
could get back again. But some risks are attractive,
and he liked the idea of descending from desolate
mountains into the heart of the enemy's defenses.

It was this stretch of the march which cost him
28 hours of continuous struggle against the wind and
snow. Up till then, he had never been far from the
coast, and he had never been able to see more than the
foothills of the island. The sea had always been there
on his left to guide him. But now he entered a long
deep valley, into the barren wilderness of peaks which
the map had dismissed so glibly. Above him, especially on the right, there were hanging valleys and
glimpses of couloirs, inscrutable and dark and silent,
and of snow cornices on their crests. To the left was the
range of crags called Soltinder, among which he somehow had to find the col which would lead him to
Bjorneskar.

Into these grim surroundings he advanced slowly

and painfully. Here and there in the valley bottom
were frozen lakes where the going was hard and
smooth; but between them the snow lay very deep, and
it covered a mass of boulders, and there he could not
tell as he took each step whether his foot would fall
upon rock or ice, or a snow crust which would support him, or whether it would plunge down hip deep
into the crevices below. Sometimes a single yard of
progress was an exhausting effort in itself, and he
would have to pause and rest for a minute after dragging himself out of a hidden hole, and look back at the
ridiculously little distance he had won. When he
paused, he was aware of his solitude. The whole valley
was utterly deserted. For mile upon mile there was no
trace of life whatever, no sign that a man had ever
been there before him, no tracks of animals, no movement or sound of birds.

Through this solemn and awful place he walked
for the whole of a night and the whole of a day, and
at dusk on the third of April he came to the top of
the col in the Soltinder, four days after Toftefjord.
Below him he saw three houses, which he knew must
be Bjorneskar, and beyond them the final sound; and
on the other side, at last, the mainland. He staggered
down the final slope to throw himself on the kindness
of Einar Sörensen.

He need never have had any doubt of his reception. Einar and his wife and his two little boys all
made him welcome, as if he were an old friend and an
honored guest. Their slender rations were brought out
and laid before him, and it was not till he had eaten
all he could that Einar took him aside to another room
to talk.

To Einar's inevitable question, Jan answered without thinking that he had heard of his name in England,
though he had really only heard it the day before. At
this, Einar said with excitement, "Did they really get
through to England?" Jan knew then that this was not
the first time escapers had been to that house. He said
he did not know whether they had reached England or

only got to Sweden, but at least their report had got through.

After this, there was no limit to what Einar was willing to do. Jan felt ashamed, when he came to think of it later, to have deceived this man on even so small a point. But the fact is that a secret agent's existence, whenever he is at work, is a lie from beginning to end; whatever he says is said as a means to an end, and the truth is a thing he can seldom tell. The better the agent is, the more thorough are his lies. He is trained with such care to shut away truth in a dark corner of his mind that he loses his natural instinct to tell the truth, for his own sake, on the few occasions when it can do no harm. Yet when, through habit, he has told an unnecessary lie to a friend, it would often involve impossible explanations to put the thing right. So Jan left Einar with the belief that whoever it was he had helped had got somewhere through to safety.

They sat for an hour that night and talked things over. Einar thought Jan should move at once. His house was the telegraph office as well as the telephone exchange, and people were in and out of it all day; and there were German camps within a mile in two directions. As for crossing the sound, there was no time better than the present. It was a dirty night, which was all to the good. The patrol boats ran for shelter whenever the weather was bad, and falling snow played havoc with the searchlights. The wind was rising, and it might be worse before the morning.

About midnight, Einar went to fetch his old father who lived in the house next door; he thought it would take two of them to row over the sound that night. Before he went out, he took Jan to the kitchen to wait. The two boys were still there with their mother, though they should surely have been in bed. They asked Jan to tell them a story, and he sat down by the fire and the younger one climbed on his knee. He was deadly tired, and he was sick at heart because the boys' father had just told him the terrible story of what had happened to Per and Eskeland and all his other companions. He put out of his mind this story of murder and treachery, and put his arm around the boy to support him, and tried to think back to his own childhood.

"Well, once upon a time," he began slowly, "in a far away country, long ago . . ."

5

The Tragedy in Tromsö

Einar had come back that afternoon from a visit to
Tromsö. Everyone there had been talking of Toftefjord
and its sequel; and although the people were used to
brutality, they were aghast at the pitiless drama which
had reached its grim climax in their town. In fact, what
Einar told Jan that night is a somber story of inhu-
manity. It is told here not because there is pleasure in
telling it, but because without it the full contrasting picture cannot be drawn of the compassion and kindliness
of the people who helped the only survivor; for all
of them were familiar with the German technique of
occupation and knew quite well what punishment they
would suffer if they were caught.

Although Einar, and everyone else in north Norway, knew the outline of the story a day or two after it
happened, it was not till the end of the war that its details were discovered. They were given then in evidence
in trials in Norwegian courts.

When the shopkeeper made the fateful decision
after his sleepless night and telephoned to his friend
the official, the official himself was faced with a dilemma. He was a member of the Norwegian Nazi party,
whose leader Quisling had been appointed head of the
puppet government by the Germans; but this fact did
not mean in itself that he had Nazi inclinations. Soon
after the occupation of Norway began many people in

minor government posts received a circular letter from
the Germans simply saying that unless they joined the
party they would be dismissed from office. In the
south, a lot of them were able to consult each other
when they got this ultimatum, and they agreed to reject
it. So many refused to join that they succeeded in calling the Germans' bluff and retained their offices. But
in the scattered districts of the north, where it might
be two days' journey for one of them to visit another,
each of them had to face this problem on his own; and
a great many of them decided, or persuaded themselves, rightly or wrongly, that if they did sign on as
members they would be able to protect the interests of
the people, whereas if they refused they would be re-
placed by a German nominee. The man the shopkeeper
knew was one of these.

In any case, Nazi or not, it was certainly his
nominal duty, as a government servant, to report any
story so strange as the one which the shopkeeper told
him that morning. Perhaps he did it unwillingly. Perhaps he argued that already a dozen people had heard
it, and that now the shopkeeper had begun to talk
there was nothing to stop him telling everyone. Moreover, the shopkeeper had told it to him on the telephone, and most of the telephones there were on party
lines. Anyone could listen to interesting conversations,
and everyone did. The story was bound to spread, and
the Germans were bound to hear it; and then the official himself would be the first to suffer.

At all events, as soon as the shopkeeper had rung
off, the official put in a call to Tromsö. With what feelings he did it, nobody but himself will ever know.

First he rang the police station, but it was still
early in the morning and the constable on duty wrote
down the report and said he would show it to his chief
at half-past nine. He also rang a friend of his in Ribbenesöy, to ask him if he had seen any strangers, and
if there was really a boat in Toftefjord. This friend
had not seen anything himself; but the shopkeeper had
just rung him up and told him all about it. Then the
official, feeling perhaps that things were moving too

quickly for him, put in a call to police headquarters. He was given another rebuff. They told him to take his own boat and go over to Toftefjord to see if the story was true.

This idea did not attract him in the least, so he called his assistant and told him to do it. The assistant went off to borrow a boat from a neighbor, but as he had not had his breakfast he sat down to a cup of coffee with the neighbor before he embarked. In the meantime the official was struck by a better idea, and rang up his friend in Ribbenesöy again and asked him to go overland to see if there was anything in Tofte-fjord. The friend said he was too old to go climbing at that time in the morning. But he sent a small boy; and sometime in the forenoon, unknown to the *Brattholm*'s crew, the boy peered over the crest of the hills and saw the top of a mast in Toftefjord, and did not dare to go nearer, and ran home to confirm the story.

When he heard this, the official rang the police headquarters again. He could assure them now that the boat had really been seen, and he hoped they agreed that there was no point in his going unarmed to investigate. He thought they should tell the Gestapo. But they rang off without giving him any definite answer; and sometime in the morning, he rang the Gestapo himself.

It seems clear when one reads this story, with its incongruous elements of inefficiency and farce, that all the Norwegian police prevaricated on purpose. No doubt they hoped that if they delayed the report for an hour or two it would help the strangers in Toftefjord, whoever they were, to make good their escape. But as the crew of the *Brattholm* did not know they had been betrayed, this effort to help them was wasted. It is said that at the very moment when the German ship was sighted off Toftefjord two rowboats were entering the fjord to warn the *Brattholm*. One of them was probably manned by the two fishermen who were going to hide the cargo, but nobody knows who was in the other one. In any case, they were too late. Both of them stopped when the German ship bore down on them,

and the men in them put out lines and pretended to be
fishing.

The people of Tromsö knew nothing of the fight
till the German ship got back there. Then they saw
prisoners being landed, and men carried ashore on
stretchers. Within a few hours, the story was whispered
throughout the town, and some hundreds of citizens
were in fear of their safety.

Tromsö claims to be the biggest town in the Arctic,
and it is the metropolis of an enormous area; but for
all that, it is not very big: about the size of an average
English market town. It is so far from other towns that
it is more than usually self-contained. It would be an
exaggeration to say that everyone knows everyone
else; but certainly everyone knows its more prominent
people. Its interests are fishing and whaling and arctic
furs, and the general business of a small seaport.
During the occupation, its modest and peaceful affairs
were swamped by the demands of a German headquarters, and its society was riven by the chasms of
political beliefs. It had its few traitors, despised and
ostracized by everybody else; and it had a new form of
society, in which money counted for very little, united
by an implacable loathing of Germans which was never
experienced in England or America.

By the time that the *Brattholm* landed, the town
had already organized itself to combat the effects of
the occupation as well as it could. Active opposition
had been out of the question without direct help from
England; there were probably more Germans than
Norwegians in north Norway. But some things could
be done, and at least preparations could be made for
the end of the occupation. Eight of the leading citizens
had combined to build up an organization to collect
intelligence and make plans to administer the town and
the surrounding country on the day of the Germans'
defeat. They expected this day from season to season
throughout the five years; each Christmas they believed it would come in the spring, and each spring
they looked forward to the autumn. They had sent

messengers to Sweden and got into touch with the free
Norwegian embassy in Stockholm, and through Stockholm with their government in London. They had been
sent a radio transmitter and it was installed in the loft
of the state hospital in the town.

Apart from sending a radio message from time to
time when the Germans did anything which seemed of
particular interest, perhaps the most important thing
which an organization of this sort could do was to be-
friend people who got into serious trouble. Many men
who would have opposed the Germans when they
found they had a chance, or when a decision was
forced upon them, had had to give in, in the early
days, for fear of what would happen to their wives and
children if they were arrested. It strengthened their
will to resist if they knew there was somebody who
would see that their families did not starve if they
themselves were imprisoned or banished to Germany.
The organization in Tromsö had this matter extremely
well arranged. It could call on funds from all the rich
people and business houses in the town. The family of
a man who suffered at the hands of the Germans was
cared for without any question. When the crisis of the
capture of *Brattholm* broke upon them, they were
actually disbursing £2000 a week in secret to widows
and orphans and the dependents of local men who had
been arrested by the Germans or forced to flee the
country.

It was never intended that the sabotage organization which the *Brattholm* party was to found should
have any connection with this existing spontaneous intelligence and relief organization. The two things were
always kept separate in Norway, so that if one was
broken open, the Germans could not necessarily pene-
trate the other. But the names of the two men in
Tromsö which had been given to Eskeland and his
party as their principal contacts were Thor Knudsen
and Kaare Moursund. These men had been chosen,
without their knowledge, merely because they were
known to be patriotic; but they were actually two of
the eight leaders of the Tromsö organization.

As soon as Jan heard from Einar in Bjorneskar that some of his companions were alive and in the Gestapo's hands, he knew that Knudsen and Moursund ought to be warned. He could not possibly go into Tromsö himself without any papers, so he asked Einar if he would do it for him. Einar agreed; but whether he ever went there is not known. If he did, he would have been too late; because both men had already been arrested.

These two arrests set Tromsö in a ferment of excitement and apprehension. Both the men were well-known in the town. Knudsen was the managing editor of one of the two local papers, and Moursund the office manager of the coastal shipping line. Knudsen was the actual man who distributed money for the organization in secret charities. Several of his colleagues in the newspaper office were involved in his illegal activities, notably the editor, whose name is Sverre Larsen, and the owner, Larsen's father, whom the Germans had already dismissed from his own paper for his views. The arrests were totally unexpected. No one believed that Knudsen or Moursund had known the *Brattholm* was coming, but it seemed only too clear that the *Brattholm*'s men had known these two names and were then, at that very moment, under Gestapo pressure. How many other names did they know? Would Knudsen and Moursund be put to torture? There was not a man in Tromsö that night with any pretentions to patriotism who did not know that his own hour might be at hand. Those who were closest to the two arrested men went home to prepare their own wives for a parting which it was useless to pretend would not be final, and to prepare themselves for the sudden imperious hammering on the door, and for the crippling pain which had to be borne in silence.

Meanwhile, the shopkeeper and the official were called to town and courteously fêted by the Germans. Neither of these somewhat simple men was any match for the questioning at which the Gestapo were so remarkably skillful whether they used torture or threats or flattery. It is very unlikely that they hid anything which they knew, whether they wanted to or not. They were thanked by the Germans, and congratulated on their excellent work, and rewarded with money and food and cigarettes and two dozen bottles of brandy. It may be supposed that there in the town they first felt the depth of the wrath of their neighbors against them. The gifts of the Germans perhaps had a bitter taste.

The next people to be arrested were, unexpectedly, the two fishermen who had promised to hide the cargo. Nobody ever discovered who had given their names to the Germans. The shopkeeper denied it. There is a possibility that the names were extracted from the crew, or that the two men were caught and questioned when they were rowing into Toftefjord, and gave themselves away. It was hard that these men were taken, because they did not even know that the cargo had come from England.

The state of tension in Tromsö did not last very much longer. While it lasted, it was in all truth hardly bearable, and it could not have been sustained for very long. During the day after the first arrests, the men who had every reason to expect to be among the next to go went on with their business as usual, because to have done anything else would have focused suspicion on themselves. The newspaper had to be written and printed, to take a single example. But it was hardly possible for them to give the appearance of normal living, or to keep their thoughts or their eyes away from the shuttered windows of the great gray Gestapo building in the middle of the town, where they knew their own names might be shouted aloud when agony went at last beyond endurance.

On the third day the news became known that the *Brattholm* men were dead and Knudsen and Moursund deported. It seems callous to say that the news of these deaths was heard with relief, and it is true that the thought of the barbarous deeds which had been done in their town shocked the townspeople profoundly; but the men themselves could only have wished that their end would come quickly.

Exactly what was done with them did not become

known till after the war was over, when their bodies
were exhumed for Christian burial and their executioners were put on trial.

Of the twelve men of the expedition, Jan had
escaped, and one man had been killed in the fight in
Toftefjord. The other ten were all brought to Tromsö
alive, although several of them were wounded. Eight
of them were shot chained together on the outskirts of
the town, and thrown into a common grave. The other
two were tortured to the point of death and then put
in the Catholic hospital, where they died.

The details of these executions are known, but
they are not a thing to be written or read about. Two
men were selected for torture in the hope that they
would talk; but the shooting of the other eight was
accompanied by acts of ferocity which were absolutely
aimless. Countries which are civilized and yet have re-
course to execution have evolved the convention of
the firing squad and the one or two blank rounds.
This protects the conscience of people whose duty
compels them to act as executioners. The method the
Germans used in Tromsö was the very opposite of this.
Yet it was done in strictest secrecy. There was no question of making use of cruelty as a deterrent to other
people. It can only have been done as it was for one
possible reason: to amuse the executioners. The Germans made it an orgy of hideous delight.

It is not known whether one of the men who
were tortured gave Knudsen's and Moursund's names
to the torturers. It would not be surprising if they did,
and no one would have the right to blame them. But it
is equally possible that the activities of these two men
were already known to the Germans, and that they
were arrested on mere suspicion of complicity in the
Brattholm affair. Both of them died in concentration
camps in Germany, and so did the two fishermen
Andreasson and Kristiansen.

So when the shopkeeper played for safety, and
the official did what he afterward claimed was his duty,
their actions cost fifteen lives. Yet it is not for an En-
glishman, who has never lived under the rule of the

Germans, to pass judgment on what they did. Their own countrymen judged them hardly. In a few moments of panic, they both threw away their peace of mind forever. For the rest of the war, their lives were made a misery by their neighbors, and after it ended, the shopkeeper was sentenced by a Norwegian court to eight years' hard labor, and the official to fourteen.

6

The Avalanche

When Einar left Jan in the kitchen at Bjorneskar and went to fetch his father, Bernhard Sörensen, the old man was in bed. Einar called to him from the bottom of the stairs, and when he woke up and asked what the matter was, he said, "Come out, Father. I want to talk to you." He was not sure if he ought to tell his mother.

Bernhard, who was 72 at that time, came down and listened to Einar's story, leaving his wife upstairs. When he had heard it all, he went back to his bedroom and began to put on his clothes. Fru Sörensen asked him where he was going.

"We've got to take the boat out," the old man said. "There's a man who wants to cross the sound."

"But now, at this time of night?" she asked him.

"Yes," he said.

"It's a terrible night."

"So much the better. We'll go down to Glomma and cross with the wind. Now, don't worry. He must get across, you see. It's one of those things we mustn't talk about."

When he was ready he left her, with no more reassurance than that, to the traditional role of women in a war. She spent an anxious night at home, waiting for Bernhard, to whom she had then been married for fifty years.

71

But he was enjoying himself. Jan had been worried at asking a man of his age to cross the sound on such a night of wind and snow. It was a row of ten miles across and back. But Bernhard laughed at his fears. When he was a young man, he had rowed to the Lofoten fishing and back every year, and that was two hundred miles. He did not think much of the rising generation. "In my day," he used to say, "it was wooden ships and iron men, and what is it now? Iron ships and a lot of wooden men. Why, do you know," he said, as they went down to the boathouse at the water's edge, "do you know, there was a young fellow taken to hospital sick only the other day. And do you know why he was sick? Because he'd got his feet wet. Yes," he chuckled, "taken to hospital because he'd got his feet wet. I've had my feet wet for over seventy years. Come along, boy. Across the sound is nothing. We'll swindle the devils out of one corpse, eh?"

The old man's good humor was catching, and Jan himself was elated at the prospect of reaching the mainland. The news of the fate of his friends had not shocked him very deeply in itself. Like everyone who took part in that kind of operation, they had all left England with a small expectation of life, and death loses its power to hurt when it is half-expected. Besides, he had thought of them as dead ever since he had seen them lying on the beach in Toftefjord. It distressed him more to learn they were captured alive and had lived for another three days, because for their own sakes and from every point of view it would have been better if they had been killed in action.

But apart from the matter of emotion, the story had a minor lesson to teach him. Hitler himself had just issued an order that everyone who took any part in this kind of guerrilla action was to be shot, whether he was in uniform or not. They had all known this before they left England; but if the order was meant to be a deterrent, it was accepted as a compliment. So far as Jan knew, this was the first time since the order was made that a crew had been captured, and he had still had a half-formed belief that a uniform might give some protection. He was still dressed as a sailor himself; but now it seemed rather absurd, on the face of it, to try to cross Norway in such a conspicuous rig. But to change it was easier thought of than done. It had been simple enough to swap underclothes with the Pedersen family, but it was different to ask someone to give him a whole civilian outfit when he had nothing to give in exchange and no money to offer. But anyhow, when he came to think of it carefully, it could not make very much difference. The Germans knew he was still at large, and he could never pass himself off as a local civilian without his civilian papers. If he kept out of sight of the Germans, his uniform did not matter, and if he came to close quarters with them, he would have to fight it out whatever clothes he was wearing. In the middle distance, the uniform might be a disadvantage; but on the other hand, he thought to himself, it was warm.

But at the particular moment when they got into the boat and took up the oars, the naval uniform was an embarrassment, because Einar and Bernhard took it for granted that he was a naval rating, and he felt that he ought to offer to row. He had rowed before, but only on lakes when he was trout fishing; and when he tried one of the heavy sweeps in the high sea which was running off Bjorneskar, all he managed to do was to knock the tops off the waves and splash the old man who was sitting astern. He had to make the lame excuse that he was too tired, and Bernhard took over, probably not surprised to find that the navy was not what it had been.

Bernhard referred to the Germans as devils. Devil is one of the few serious swear words in the Norwegian language, but he used it with a lack of emphasis that made it rather engaging. It was as if he could not bring himself to utter the word German. "You see the point of land over there?" he would say to Jan. "That's Finkroken. There are seventy devils there. They've some damned great cannons, and searchlights. We'll give them a wide berth. And down there ahead of us, that's Sjursnes. That's where the patrol boats lie. A whole company of devils there too. But don't you worry. They won't get you this time, boy. We'll swindle them. We'll steer between them." And he chuckled with joy, and heaved on his massive oar.

Jan was more than content to leave it to Einar and Bernhard to get him across the sound. This was the second consecutive night he had been without sleep, and he had been on the go all the time. He was too tired to take any notice of the flurries of snow and spindrift, or the steep seas which bore down on them out of the darkness to starboard, or of the searchlights which endlessly swept the sound and sometimes appeared as a dazzling eye of light with a halo around it when a beam passed over them. Einar and his father were sure they would not be seen, so long as the snow went on falling, and they were not bothered about the patrol boats, although they were crossing their beats. "No devils at sea on a night like this," the old man said. "There's not a seaman among them."

Jan did not care. The mainland was close ahead, and Einar had given him the things which he coveted most in the world just then: a pair of ski boots and skis. In an hour or so, he would finish with boats and the sea, and enter a medium where he would feel at home. Among the snow mountains on skis he would be confident of outdistancing any German. He could go where he wished and depend upon no one. Even the Swedish frontier was only sixty miles away: two days' journey, if all went well; and the Germans had lost his trail. He needed one good sleep, he thought, and then he would be his own master.

It was about three in the morning when Bernhard and Einar beached the boat on the southern shore. Jan jumped out thankfully. The others could not afford to wait. To take advantage of the wind on the way back home, they would have to row close under the devils' gun battery at Finkroken. They thought they could bluff it out if they were seen, so long as they were not too far away from home, but it would be better not to have to try. So as soon as Jan was ashore with his skis, they wished him luck and pushed off and disappeared: two more to add to this list of chance acquaintances to whom he owed his life.

There were small farms along the water's edge just there, with houses spaced out at intervals of two hundred yards or so. The people who owned them pastured sheep and cattle on the narrow strip of fertile land between the sea and the mountainside, and eked out a living by fishing. The Sörensens knew everyone who lived there, and had said he could go safely to any of the houses. They had specially mentioned a man called Lockertsen. He lived in a farm called Snarby, which was a little larger than the rest, and he had a thirty-foot motorboat which might come in useful.

Jan would gladly have set off there and then without making further contacts. He felt guilty already at the number of people he had involved in his own predicament; and besides, this series of short encounters, each at a high pitch of excitement and emotion, was exhausting in itself. He longed to be able to sleep in barns without telling anyone, and take to the hills again each morning. But before he was fit to embark on a life like that, he had to have one long sleep whatever it cost him, and that night he could only count on a few hours more before the farms were stirring. He reluctantly put his skis on his shoulder and went up through a steep farmyard to the house which was nearest. He crept quietly around the house till he found the door, and he tried the handle. It opened. As it happened, this was Snarby.

Fru Lockertsen said afterward it was the first night she had forgotten to lock the door since the occupation started. In ordinary times, of course, nobody thought of keys in a place like that; it was not once in a year that a stranger came to the door. But now, when you could always see a German patrol ship from the front windows of Snarby, you felt better at nights behind a good lock; and when she was woken by blundering footsteps in the kitchen, the first thing she thought was that some German sailors had landed. She prodded her

husband and whispered that there was somebody in the
house, and he listened, and dragged himself out of bed,
and went to see what was happening.

Lockertsen was a big heavily built man like a polar
bear. He was a head taller than Jan and looked as
though he could have picked him up and crushed him;
and probably that is what he felt inclined to do. He was
intensely suspicious. Jan told him his story, and then
told it all over again, but every time he told it Lockertsen had thought of new doubts and new questions. He
simply refused to believe it, and Jan could not understand why. But the fact is that Jan was so sleepy that
he hardly knew what he was saying. His explanation
was muddled and unconvincing, and the way he told
the story made it sound like a hastily invented lie. The
only thing that was still quite clear in his head was that
he must not say where he had come from. Somebody
had brought him across from Ringvassöy, he insisted;
but he refused to say who it was and could not explain
why he refused to say it. To Lockertsen one naval uniform was probably much the same as another, and Jan
had obviously landed from the sound; and the only navy
in the sound was German. It seemed much more likely
that he was a German deserter. Even the toe would have
fitted that explanation. Everyone had heard of self-in-
flicted wounds.

The argument went on for a solid hour, and it
only ended then because Jan could not talk any longer.
His speech had got slow and blurred. He had to sleep.
It was a pity, and he was resentful that the man did not
believe him. But he was finished. He had taxed his
endurance too much, and left himself without the
strength to get away. Let him report him if he liked;
there was nothing more to be done about it. He lay
down on the rug in front of the kitchen stove. He
heard Lockertsen say, "All right. You can stay there
till half-past five." At that, he fell deeply asleep.

Lockertsen spent the rest of the night pacing up
and down the kitchen and trying to puzzle things out,
and stopping from time to time to look down at the defenseless, mysterious creature asleep on his floor.

Many of the doubts which had afflicted the shopkeeper came to him also, and they were strengthened for him by the fact that the stranger had come from a place where he knew there were Germans. But Lockertsen was a man of different caliber. He had plenty of courage. He was only determined to get the truth out of Jan, if he had to do it by force. He was not going to act one way or the other until he was sure.

Some time while Jan was sleeping the big man went down on his knees on the hearthrug and searched through his pockets. There was nothing in them which gave him a clue, and Jan did not stir.

He had said he could sleep till 5:30, and at 5:30 he shook him awake. The result of this surprised him. Jan was subconsciously full of suspicion, and leapt to his feet and drew his automatic and Lockertsen found himself covered before he could move.

"Take it easy, take it easy," he said in alarm. "Everything's all right." Jan looked around him and saw that the kitchen was empty, and grinned and said he was sorry.

"You can't lie there all day," Lockertsen said. "The wife'll be wanting to cook. But I've made up my mind. You can go up in the loft and have your sleep out, and then we'll see what's to be done with you."

Jan gratefully did as he told him; and when he woke again in the middle of the day, refreshed and capable of explaining himself, Lockertsen's distrust of him soon disappeared. Fru Lockertsen and their daughter fed him and fussed over him, and Lockertsen himself grew amiable and asked him where he was going. Jan answered vaguely, "Over the mountains," and Lockertsen offered to take him part of his way in the motorboat if that would help him.

Jan's idea of where he was going was really rather vague. By that time, by a process of subconscious reasoning, he had decided to make for Sweden. He knew he ought to tell London what had happened. At headquarters they would soon be expecting signals from his party's transmitter, and they would already be waiting for *Brattholm* to get back to Shetland. In a week or

two they would give her up as lost, and when no signals
were heard they would probably guess that the whole
party had been lost at sea. No one would ever know,
unless he told them, that he was alive, and sooner or
later, in the autumn perhaps, they would send another
party. It would really be stupid for him to try to work
on alone when nobody in England knew he was there.
Any work he could do might clash with a second party's
plans. The proper thing for him to do, he could see,
was to get into Sweden and fly back to England and
join the second party when it sailed.

To go to Sweden was a simple aim. If he kept moving south, he would be bound to get there in the end.
But nobody he had met had had a map, even of the
most misleading sort, and he could only plan his route
from recollection. He was now on the very end of one
of the promontories between the great fjords which
run deep into the northern mountains. To the west of
him was Balsfjord, and to the east Ullsfjord and then
Lyngenfjord, the greatest of them all, fifty miles long
and three miles wide. All the promontories between
these fjords are high and steep. The one between Ullsfjord and Lyngenfjord in particular is famous for its
mountain scenery: it is a mass of jagged peaks of fantastic beauty which rise steeply from the sea on either
side. Away from their shores, these promontories are
not only uninhabited, they are deserted, never visited at
all except in summer and in peace time by a few moun-
taineers and by Lapps finding pasture for their reindeer. Along the shores there are scattered houses, and
roads where there is room to build them.

Jan's choice of route was simplified by the fact that
Tromsö lay to the west of him, and the farther he
went that way the thicker the German defenses would
become. Apart from that, he had to decide whether to
keep to the fjords and make use of roads when he could
find them, or to cut himself off from all chance of
meeting either friend or enemy by staying in the hills.

Lockertsen's advice was definite. On the shores of
the fjords he would run the risk of meeting Germans,
which would be awkward; but to cross the mountains

alone at that time of year was, quite simply, impossible
and suicidal, and nobody but a lunatic would try it.

They talked all around the subject several times.
Jan listened to everything that Lockertsen suggested, in-
tending as usual to take the advice which suited him and
forget about the rest. In the upshot, Lockertsen said
he would take him in his motorboat that night as far as
he could up Ullsfjord, and land him on the far shore,
the eastward side. There was a road there which ran
up a side fjord called Kjosen and crossed over to Lyngenfjord through a gap in the mountains. Then it ran
all the way to the head of Lyngenfjord; and from
there there was both a summer and a winter road
which led to the frontier. It was true that the road itself might not be much use of him. It ran through several small villages on the fjord, which would be sure to
have garrisons. Beyond the end of the fjord, the summer road of course would be buried in snow and the
winter road, which crossed the frozen lakes, was certainly blocked and watched by the Germans. But at
least this was a line to follow, and it skirted around
the mountains.

Jan hated the thought of putting to sea again, but
the lift he was offered would put him twenty miles on
his way, and he accepted it. When it was dark, he said
good-bye to Fru Lockertsen and her daughter and went
down to the shore again. Lockertsen rowed him out to
the motorboat, which was lying at a buoy, and a neighbor joined them. There was fishing gear on board, and
Lockertsen and the neighbor meant to use it, when they
landed Jan, to give themselves a reason for the journey.
They started her up and cast off, and put out once
more into the dangerous waters of the sound.

Jan made them keep close inshore, so that if they
were suddenly challenged by a German ship he could
go over the side and swim to land. So they crept up
the sound under the shadow of the mountains. But
nothing happened; they slipped safely around the corner into Ullsfjord, and in the early hours of the morning put Jan ashore on a jetty at the mouth of Kjosen.

Neither Lockertsen's warning, nor the maps and

photographs he had studied, nor even the fame of the
Lyngen Alps had quite prepared Jan for the sight which
he saw when he landed at Kjosen. It was still night, but
ahead of him in the east the sky was pale; and there
were the mountains, a faint shadow on the sky where
the rock was naked, a faint gleam where it was clothed
with snow. Peak upon peak hung on the breathless air
before the dawn, immaculate and sublime. Beneath
their majesty, the enmity of Germans seemed something to be despised.

He saw the road, beside the shining ribbon of the
fjord; it was the first road he had seen in all his journey.
He put on his skis with a feeling of exaltation and
turned toward the frontier. The crisp hiss of skis on
the crusted snow and the rush of the frosty air was
the keenest of all possible delight. He knew of the
danger of garrisons in the villages on the road, and he
knew that the largest of them was only five miles ahead,
but at that time and in that place it seemed absurd to
cower in fear of Germans. He determined to push on
and get through the village before the sun had risen or
the people were awake.

The name of the village is Lyngseidet. It lies in
the narrow gap between Kjosen and Lyngenfjord. In
peace, it is a place which cruising liners visit on their
way to North Cape. From time to time in summer they
suddenly swamp it with their hordes of tourists; the
people of the village, it is said, hurriedly send lorries to
Tromsö for stocks of furs and souvenirs, and the Lapps
who spend the summer there dress up in their best and
pose for photographs. In war time it was burdened with
a garrison of more than normal size, because it is the
point at which the main road crosses Lyngenfjord by
ferry.

Jan expected to find a roadblock on each side of
it, and probably sentries posted in the middle, but on
skis he felt sure he could climb above the road to cir-
cumvent a block, and to pass the sentries he relied on
his speed and the remaining darkness.

He came to the roadblock, just as he had foreseen.
It was a little way short of the head of the fjord at

Kjosen. There was a pole across the road, and a hut beside it which presumably housed a guard. He struck off the road up the steep hillside to the left. As he had thought, on skis it was quite easy; but it took longer than he expected, because there were barbed wire fences which delayed him. One of his ski bindings was loose as well, and he had to stop for some time to repair it. When he got down to the road again a couple of hundred yards beyond the roadblock, it was fully daylight.

He pushed on at top speed along the road. He knew it could not be more than two or three miles to the village, and he ought to be through it in ten or fifteen minutes. It was getting risky, but it was worth it; to have stopped and hidden where he was would have wasted the whole of a day, and the thought of the distance he might cover before the evening was irresistible. There was a little twist in the road where it rounded a mass of rock, and beyond it he could already see the roofs of houses. He turned the corner at a good speed.

Fifty yards ahead was a crowd of German soldiers. They straggled across the road and filled it from side to side. There was not time to stop or turn and no place to hide. He went on. More and more of them came from a building on the left: twenty, thirty, forty. He hesitated for a fraction of a second but his own momentum carried him on toward them, and no challenge came, no call to halt. They were carrying mess tins and knives and forks. Their uniforms were unbuttoned. He shot in among them, and they stood back to right and left to let him pass, and for a moment he looked full into their faces and saw their sleepy eyes and smelled the frowsty, sweaty smell of early morning. Then he was past, so acutely aware of the flag and the NORWAY on his sleeves that they seemed to hurt his shoulders. He fled up the road, expecting second by second and yard by yard the shouts and the hue and cry. At the turn of the road he glanced over his shoulder, and they were still crossing the road and going into a house on the other side, and not one of them looked his way. A second later, he was out of sight.

The road went uphill through a wood of birch, and he pounded up it without time to wonder. After a mile he came to the top of the rise. The valley opened out, and ahead he saw the village itself, and the spire of the church, and the wide water of Lyngenfjord beyond it, and the road which wound downhill and vanished among the houses. He thrust with his sticks once more,

and began a twisting run between the fences of the road. He knew he would come to a fork at the bottom, in the middle of the village. The left-hand turning ran a little way down Lyngenfjord toward the sea and then came to an end; it was the right-hand one which led to the head of the fjord and then to the frontier. He passed the first of the houses, going fast. The church was on the right of the road and close to the water's edge. There was a wooden pier behind it, and down by the church-yard fence where the road divided a knot of men was standing.

A moment passed before he took in what he saw. Two or three of the men were soldiers, and one was a civilian who stood facing the others. Behind them was another pole across the road, and one of the soldiers was turning over some papers in his hand.

About five seconds more would have halted him among them at the roadblock, but there was a gate on the right which led to a garage in a garden and it was open. He checked and turned and rushed through the gate and around the garage and up the steep garden and headed for some birch scrub behind it. There were shouts from the crossroad, and as he came out into view of it again beyond the garage two or three rifle shots were fired, but he reached the bushes and set himself to climb the mountainside.

In Toftefjord when the Germans were behind him, he had been afraid, but now he was elated by the chase. With a Norwegian's pride in his skill on skis, he knew they could not catch him. He climbed up and up, exulting in the skis and his mastery of them, and hearing the futile shouts grow distant in the valley down below. He looked back, and saw a score of soldiers struggling far behind him up his trail. He passed the treeline and went on, up onto the open snow above.

Up there, he met the sunshine. The sun was rising above the hills on the far side of Lyngenfjord. The water below him sparkled in its path, and in the frosty morning air the whole of the upper part of the fjord was visible. On the eastern side and at the head he could see the curious flat-topped hills which are the outliers of the great plateau through which the frontier runs; and far up at the end of the fjord, fifteen miles away, was the valley called Skibotten up which the frontier road begins. To see his future route stretched out before him added to the joy he already felt at having left the valleys and the shore: he was almost glad of the accident which had forced him to grasp the danger of taking to the hills. And seeing the fjord so beautifully displayed below him had brought back his recollection of the map. There had been a dotted line, he now remembered, which ran parallel to the road and to the shore. This marked a summer track along the face of the mountains; and although it was the same

map as the one of Ringvassöy, and the track had probably been put in from hearsay and not surveyed, yet if
it had ever been possible to walk that way in summer, it
ought to be possible now to do it on skis in snow. At
least, there could not be any completely impassable
precipice, and so long as the fjord was in sight he could
not lose his way.

He stopped climbing after about 3000 feet, and
rested and looked around him. The pursuit had been
given up, or fallen so far behind that he could not see or
hear it; and up there everything was beautiful and calm
and peaceful. At that height he was almost level with
the distant plateau, and he could see glimpses here and
there beyond the fjord of mile upon mile of flat unbroken snow. But on his own side, close above him, the
mountains were much higher. He was on the flank of a
smooth conical hill with the Lappish name of Goalesvarre, and its top was still 1500 feet above him; and
behind it the main massif of the Lyngen Alps rose in a
maze of peaks and glaciers to over 6000 feet.

It was not until he rested there that he had leisure
to think of his fantastic encounter with the platoon of
soldiers. At first it had seemed incredible that they
should have taken no notice of him and let him pass;
but when he came to think it over, he saw that it
was typical of any army anywhere. It was like the search
in Ribbenesöy: one expected the German army to be
more fiendishly efficient than any other, but it was not;
or at least, not always. He could imagine a British or
Norwegian platoon, or an American one for that matter, shut away in a dreary post like that, with nothing
whatever to do except guard a road and a ferry where
nothing ever happened. With one section on guard at
the roadblock, the others, to say the least of it, would
never be very alert, and just after reveille they would
not be thinking of anything much except breakfast.
If someone in a queer uniform came down the road, the
guard must have let him through, they would say, and
that was the guard's funeral. The officers would know
all about it, anyway, whoever he was. Nobody would
want to make a fool of himself by asking officious ques-

tions. And the uniform itself, Jan reflected, would have meant nothing to them in a foreign country. Probably none of them knew that the word NORWAY was English, any more than you would expect an English soldier to know the German word for Norway. For all they knew or cared, he might have been a postman or a sanitary inspector on his rounds; anything was more likely, far inland, than meeting an enemy sailor on skis. Sooner or later, one of them might mention it to an n.c.o., who might pull the leg of the corporal of the guard next time he saw him, and by the evening perhaps it would come to the ears of the platoon commander, who certainly would not want to report it and would spend a lot of time questioning his men to prove to himself that it was really nothing important.

But of course the guard on the roadblock in Lyngseidet was a more unfortunate encounter. They certainly knew he was up to something illegal, because he had run away, and they knew fairly exactly where he had gone. That incident was bound to be reported, at least to battalion headquarters. He could not be sure if they had seen the uniform, or whether headquarters would put two and two together and guess that the man who had been seen in Lyngseidet was the one who had escaped in Toftefjord. It depended how many other people in the district, for one reason or another, were on the run. At the worst, it meant they had picked up his trail again, and if they thought it was worth it, they might put extra patrols in the country he had to pass through. He wondered how badly they wanted to catch him.

In any case, the best thing, as ever, was speed: to travel faster than they would think he could possibly travel. And now he had the means to do this, because people who do not know much about skis can often hardly believe the distance an expert can go on them in the course of a day. The Germans would not know much about them unless they were Bavarians; and even people who ski in the Alps are inclined only to think of skiing downhill, and going uphill by lifts or even railways. Cross-country ski-running, uphill and down, is a particularly Norwegian activity, and a Norwegian skier on holiday, or merely on a journey, thinks nothing of fifty miles a day.

So Jan set off with confidence, and even with a certain amount of pleasure, in anticipation of the run. He imagined himself staying at about 3000 feet, following the contour along the fjord and keeping the water in sight. But of course no mountainside, even the side of a fjord, is quite so regular and simple. He had only gone a few miles along the slope of Goalesvarre when he found a side valley in front of him which ran deep into the mountains. As he approached it and the head of it opened up, he saw the smooth snow surface of a glacier in it, and even the glacier was below him. Rather than try to cross it, he went right down to the valley bed below the ice and climbed up it again on the other side.

Beyond the valley there was another minor hazard of a different kind. The side of the fjord became steeper, and finally sheer. To get past this cliff he might have gone over the top; but it was very high, and to the right of it, on the inland side, there was a col which seemed a more sensible line for the summer track to follow. It looked as though it would lead back to the fjord five miles or so beyond. So he headed for the col, and very soon he lost sight of the fjord.

By then it must have been about eleven o'clock in the morning, and he had covered something like twenty miles since he left the boat at Kjosen. It was good going, and everything looked promising; but it was just before he reached the col that the weather changed again.

It came over the high summits on his right, first the white wisps of clouds like flags on the highest peaks, and then the stray gusts of wind and the darkening of the sky. The sun went in, and the snowfields lost their sparkling clarity and detail and became monotonous and gray, and the air at once struck chill. And then the snow began to fall, softly at first but more heavily minute by minute as the wind increased and the clouds descended. With the same abruptness that he had seen in Ringvassöy, the storm swooped downward and enveloped him in a whirling white impenetrable wall.

It had happened before, and it gave him no cause to be alarmed, because all the sudden storms he had seen in the last few days had been short, and had ended as suddenly as they had begun. It was annoying, the more so now that he had skis. In his rubber boots the storms had not made much difference to his speed. He had plodded on all through them. But now he could not make use of his extra speed. He could hardly see five yards in front of him, and any slight downward grade might lead to a sudden drop. He had to be able to stop at any moment, and on slopes which he might have run at full speed he now had to check, and creep down circumspectly. It was not only slow, it was twice as tiring.

Nevertheless, he pressed on, hoping and still expecting to see the lightening of the cloud which would be the sign that the squall was passing and that a few minutes more would bring sunshine again with the snowcloud whirling away toward the fjord.

But no sign came. On the contrary, the wind went on increasing. It was getting worse than anything he had experienced before, and as hours passed he had to admit to himself that this was not merely a squall. It was useless to rely upon its ending. He ought to act as though it might last for days. That meant that he must find shelter, and to find it he must get down to the fjord again.

But before he had come unwillingly to this decision, a new aspect of the storm began to be manifest. The surface of the lying snow began to creep, first in whorls and eddies, and later in clouds which forced him to shut his eyes and put his hand over his mouth to keep the driving snow powder out of his throat and lungs. When the very surface he stood on began to move, there was nothing stable left for his eyes to be fixed upon; when he stood still, the snow silted into the tracks which he had made, and then it was only by the wind that he could have any idea which direction he had been going. Each little slope which faced him then

became a new problem in itself. Each one which he saw
from the bottom vanished into the shifting mists a few
feet above his head, and each of them might be the foot
of a great mountain or the whole of a tiny mound.
From the top of a slope he could not tell whether it was
five feet in height or a thousand. He only knew that
somewhere about him the surface plunged down in
sheer chasms to the fjord waters three thousand feet
below, and that somewhere it rose three thousand feet
above him to the soaring crags he had seen in the light
of the dawn.

He guided himself by the wind, keeping it on his
right. The right side of his body was coated with ice; it
matted his hair and his week-old beard, and his right
hand grew numb. He had tried to keep on in the direction he had been going when the storm came down, because he believed it would lead him to lower ground.
But after some hours he began to doubt even the wind.
He would sometimes have sworn that he had traveled
for fifty yards in a straight line, and yet the wind
which had been on his right swooped down on him
from ahead. It seemed to be eddying down from the
higher mountains, perhaps following valleys which he
could not see. He stood still to test it, and even while
he stood still it changed direction. Without the wind to
guide him, he was lost.

Some time during that day he stopped and tried to
dig himself into the snow to wait for the abatement of
the storm, because he despaired of finding the way out
of the mountains. But as soon as he crouched down in
the little hollow he scraped out, the cold attacked him
with such violence that he knew he would die here if
he rested. He had often read that if you lie down and
sleep in a blizzard you never get up again. Now he
knew it was true: it would not take very long. He got
up and put on his skis and struggled onward, not caring
much anymore which way he was moving, but moving
because he did not dare to stop. Toward the end of
the day his wandering became quite aimless and he
lost all sense either of time or space.

One cannot say whether it was the same day or

the next that he first perceived a continuity in the
slope of the mountain. He was going downhill. By then
he had devised a plan for descending slopes which had
probably already saved his life. When he came to a
void, he gathered a big snowball and kneaded it hard
and threw it in front of him. Sometimes, above the
sound of the wind, he heard it fall, and then he went
on; but more often it vanished without any sound at all,
and he turned aside and tried another way. Now, edg-
ing cautiously down a slope and throwing snowballs, he
saw rock walls both to the right and left of it. It was a
watercourse. He knew it was possible, or even likely,
that it led to the top of a frozen waterfall and that he
was running a serious risk of stepping on to the ice of
the fall before he could see it. But at last it was something to follow which must lead in the end to the sea. He
crept down it with infinite caution, testing every step
for hidden ice. He saw little bushes and knew he was
getting low. And then, directly below him, there was a
square block which loomed dark in the snow. He ran
joyfully down the last few yards toward it, because he
thought it was a house. But it was not. It was only an
enormous isolated rock. But it had a hollow underneath
it, like a cave, and he squeezed in there, lying down
because it was not high enough to crawl. As soon as he
lay down, in shelter from the wind and snow, he went
to sleep.

That rock is the first identifiable place which Jan
came to on that journey. It stands in a narrow valley
called Lyngdalen. It is only about ten miles in a perfectly straight line from Lyngseidet, where the roadblock was: but nobody knows where or how far he had
been before he got there.

At the rock he made a mistake which was nearly
fatal. There is an acute bend in the valley just there. As
he approached it, down the northern side, the valley
led on in two directions, one only a little way to the
left and the other equally little to the right. Downstream was to the left, and that way the valley ran
without any hazard straight down to Lyngenfjord, five
miles below. To the right the valley led gently up to

the foot of the highest mountain in north Norway, the
peak of Jaeggevarre, 6200 feet high. In clear weather,
the choice is obvious; in fact, Jaeggevarre towers over
the upper valley and closes it with a sheer bastion
3000 feet high and three miles long. But in storm, when
neither the mountain nor the valley walls were visible,
the place was a trap. A great moraine nearly closes the
valley at that point. The summer river passes it through
a gorge. But in winter the gorge is full of snow, and the
immediate foreground of the valley floor slopes down
to the right, upstream. When Jan woke up and crept out
of the crevice below the rock, the storm was still
raging. He saw nothing except the foreground, and he
put on his skis again and set forth, downhill, toward the
right, away from Lyngenfjord and all possible help or
safety, into the very heart of the highest hills.

He was beginning to suffer from exposure by then,
and one cannot deduce how long he had been storm-
bound, or whether it was night or day. When one's
body is worn by a long effort at the limit of its strength,
and especially when its function is dulled by cold, one's
mind loses first of all its sharp appreciation of time.
Incidents which are really quite separate become
blended together; the present and the immediate past
are not distinct, but are all part of a vaguely defined
present of physical misery. In a person of strong character, hope for the future remains separate long after
the past and present are confused. It is when the future
loses its clarity too, and hope begins to fade, that death
is not far away.

Jan's mind was certainly numbed and confused by
then, but so far he had not the slightest doubt about
the future, and he was still thinking clearly enough to
use the commonsense of the craft of mountaineering.
Now that he had found what he knew was a river
valley of considerable size, he did not expect any trouble in following it to the sea; and so he was astonished
and baffled when he found the ground rising in front
of him again. He had come to what he thought was a
frozen lake, though in fact it is only a level part of the
valley floor, and he followed what seemed to be the

shore of it, with the valley wall above him on his right. He came to the end of it expecting to find its outflow; but there was still a steep slope above him, and he could not see the top. He went right around the lake till he came back to the moraine where he had started; and there for the second time he missed the snow-filled gorge. Search as he might, he could not find the outlet. He seemed to be in the bottom of a bowl, with the lake on his left as he circled around it and unbroken snow-slopes always on his right. There was nothing for it except to give up the hope of going on downhill. He had to start climbing again.

His choice of direction then, if it was not at random, was probably governed by the light. In the thickest of cloud and snow one sometimes has an impression of greater darkness where a steep rock face is close above. The sides of Lyngdalen may have thrown extra darkness, and so may the sharp bend downstream in the narrow valley. But upstream Jaeggevarre stands farther back, and in that direction there is less to obscure the light. Jan may have concluded that this was south, or that it was really the lower reaches of the valley. At all events, he began to climb that way. He went up diagonally, hoping and expecting all the way to find an easing of the gradient and a sign that the valley went on beyond. Very soon he lost sight of the bottom, but although he climbed on and on, he could not see the top. He was on a slope of snow which in his restricted vision seemed eternal; on his left it vanished into invisible depths, and on his right it merged in the cloud above. In front of him and behind him, it was exactly the same: his ski tracks across it disappeared a few seconds after he had made them. It was a world of its own, dizzily tilted on edge, full of the tearing wind, with himself for ever at the center and the farthest edges diffuse and ill-defined.

Suddenly with lightning speed the snow slope split from end to end and the snow below his feet gave way. He fell on his side and snatched at the surface, but everything was moving, and the snow fell upon him and rolled him over and over. He felt himself going down

and down, faster and faster, fighting with roaring masses
of snow which were burying him alive. It wrenched and
pounded his helpless body, and choked him and bat-
tered him till he was unconscious. He fell limply in the
heart of the avalanche and it cast out his body on the
valley floor below. Down there he lay still, long after its
thunder had echoed away to silence.

7

Snowblind

The next summer, somebody passed that way and found the broken pieces of Jan's skis, among the massive blocks of melting snow which were all that was left of the avalanche. They were at the foot of the icefall of the unnamed glacier under the east face of Jaeggevarre. One can guess what he had done. He had started his final climb up the valley wall, but had traversed on to the icefall without knowing it. When one can see a little distance, the snow on ice looks different from the snow on rock; but if one can only see a yard or two one cannot tell what is underneath. The snow on the steep ice at that time of year would have been very unstable, ready to fall by itself within a week or two, and Jan's weight and the thrust of his skis were enough to start it. The scar of the avalanche stretched from top to bottom of the icefall. Jan himself must have fallen at least three hundred feet.

To start an avalanche is apt to be fatal, but it did not kill Jan. Luck was extraordinarily kind to him again. Of course nobody knows how long he lay there unconscious; but when he came to, his head was out of the snow, so that he could breathe, and most of his body was buried, which had probably saved him from freezing to death; and none of his bones were broken. To be alive was far more than he had any right to expect, and so the other results of his fall can hardly be counted as bad luck. One of his skis was lost and the other was broken in two places; and the small rucksack with all his food had disappeared; and he had hit his head and could not remember where he was trying to go. He dug himself out of the snow and stood up, and unfastened the broken bit of ski and dropped it there, and wandered away on foot, utterly lost, with no plan and no notion of where he was going; in fact, without any coherent thoughts at all, because he had a concussion of the brain.

After the avalanche, Jan had no sense of time, and hardly any awareness of the reality of what happened. He never stopped walking, but as his body froze slowly and ice formed in the veins of his feet and hands and crept inch by inch up his legs and arms, his mind became occupied more and more by dreams and hallucinations. But the length of this ordeal is known: he was four days and four nights in the mountains from the time when he passed through Lyngseidet. The storm lasted for nearly three days, and then the snow stopped and the clouds lifted and the mountains were clear; but Jan knew nothing of that, because by then the glare of the snow had scorched the retina of his eyes and he was blind.

One has to imagine him, both in the dark and the daylight, and both in the mists of the storm and the clear air which followed it, stumbling on unable to see at all. He never stopped because he was obsessed with the idea that if he lay down he would go to sleep and die; but all the time he was in snow between knee-deep and waist-deep, and toward the end of the time he fell down so often full length on his face in the snow that he might be said to have crawled and not to have walked.

His movements were totally aimless. This is known because his tracks were found here and there, later on in the spring. For the most part, he probably stayed in the valley of Lyngdalen, but at least once he went over a thousand feet up the side of it, and down again in the same place. He was deflected by the smallest of obstacles. There were boulders sticking up out of the snow, and when he ran into them head-on he turned and went away; not around the boulder and on in the same direction, but away at an angle, on a totally different course. There were birch bushes also, in the bottom of the valley, and among them he wandered hither and thither for days, crossing his own tracks again and again and blundering into the bushes themselves so that he got tangled in them and scratched his face and hands and tore his clothes. Once he walked around and around a small bush for so long that he trod a hard deep path in the snow, which was still to be seen in the summer: one can only suppose that he thought he was following somebody else's footsteps.

But he himself knew almost nothing of this. Because he was blind, he believed that the mist and falling snow went on all the time, and he could not reckon the nights and days which were passing. All that he knew of reality was pain in his legs and arms and eyes, and cold and hunger, and the endless, hampering, suffocating wall of snow in front of him through which he must force his way.

On one of the mountains he came to, there were hundreds of people, marching with bare feet which were frozen and they were afraid of breaking them, because they were quite brittle.

He knew it was a dream, and he wrenched himself awake because he was terrified of falling asleep, but when Per Blindheim began to talk to him it was more real than reality, and he swung around joyfully and called "Per, Per," into the darkness because he could not see where he was. But Per did not answer him, he went on talking to Eskeland. They were talking together somewhere, and a lot of the others were with them too, but they were not listening to him. He shouted louder, "Per! Eskeland!" and began to run after them, afraid that they would miss him in the night. And then they were close, and he was thankful to be with them all again. But they were talking together among themselves, quite cheerfully as they always did, and they never spoke to him. He called them again and again to tell them he could not see, but he could not make them

hear him. They did not know he was there. And it
came back to him that all of them were dead. Yet they
had been talking together before he lost them, and he
was the one who could not make himself heard. He
began to believe that the dream was reality, and that he
was the one who was dead. Stories of death came back
into his mind. It seemed likely that he had died.

But in the same thought which made it seem so
likely, he knew it was fantasy and he was still determined not to die, and to this end he must keep going,
on and on, until something happened: something.
He could not remember what it was that he had hoped
would happen.

As he was going through the woods, he came to a
trapdoor in the snow, and he tried to open it by the
iron ring. But he was feeling very weak, and it was too
heavy for him. It was a pity, because of the warm fire
inside it, but he had to give it up. But whenever he
turned his back on it to go away, somebody slipped out
of the forest and opened it and got inside and shut it
again before he had time to stop him. It was unfair that
they kept him shut out in the cold and darkness while
they all enjoyed the lights and gaiety inside. They always waited till he turned away, and then they were
too quick for him. They must have been watching him
and waiting for their chance.

It was the same when he found the mountain with
windows in it, except that that time he never saw them
go in. But they all climbed up to the door at the top so
easily. Nobody would help him, and he tried and tried
but always slipped down again to the bottom so that he
was the only one left who could not do it. But perhaps it
was nobody's fault; perhaps the explanation was that
they could not see him. That would be logical if he was
dead. But he shouted I am still alive and alone out here
in the snow, it's all a mistake. The windows went away
and the mountain turned into a little mound of snow,
and he was scrabbling feebly at its sides.

It was the same too when he came to the log
cabin. Stupidly, he was not looking where he was going,
and he hurt himself again when he blundered into it.

But as soon as he put out his hands and felt the rough logs he knew what it was although they never told him, and he started to feel his way along the wall, around the corner, hoping they would not see him before he found the door. It seemed a long way to the door, but he found it, and felt for the latch. But that time it opened, and he fell inside.

8

Marius

Hanna Pedersen was having dinner with her two boys, Ottar and Johan, when the door burst open and the dreadful thing stumbled into the room and groped blindly toward the table. They jumped to their feet and backed away in horror. She nearly screamed, but she put her hand to her mouth and stifled the impulse because of the children. She managed to whisper, "Ottar, go and fetch your uncle," and the elder boy slipped out of the room.

"What do you want?" she said. "Who are you?" But Jan's answer was incoherent, and he collapsed on the floor. She overcame her terror and revulsion enough then to creep near him and look at him closely to see if he was somebody she knew.

It would have been hard to tell. When he lay still like that on the floor, one would have thought he was a corpse dug out of the snow. He was caked with ice and frozen dirt and dried blood. His hair and his beard were solidly frozen and his face and hands were bloated and discolored. His feet were great balls of compacted snow and ice. His eyes were shut tight, screwed up with the pain of snowblindness. He tried to speak again as he lay there, but she could not understand anything he said. Distracted with fright she took the smaller boy and ran to the door to meet her brother.

Her brother's name was Marius Grönvold. He

lived in the next house, and when he heard the boy's anxious frightened story he ran across to see what had really happened. He pushed past his sister and took a single look at Jan. It was enough to show him that they would have to take measures quickly, whoever this man was, if they were to save his life. He had two other sisters who lived nearby, Gudrun and Ingeborg, and he sent the children to fetch them. They both hurried in, and between them all they set to work to bring Jan back to life. They built up the fire, and fed him with hot milk from a spoon, and got off the worst of his clothes and wrapped him in blankets, and lifted him onto a bed. Marius took a sharp knife and carefully cut his boots to pieces and peeled them off. His socks also had to be cut up and taken off in strips, revealing horrible feet and legs in an advanced stage of frostbite, with the toes frozen stiffly together in a solid block of ice. Everyone there knew the first aid treatment for a frostbite: to rub it with snow. The three sisters started then and there to try to save his feet, taking the ice cold limbs between their hands and kneading the brittle flesh. Jan paid no attention to what they did, because he could not feel anything in his legs at all. He seemed to be slipping off into sleep or unconsciousness.

When the ice began to thaw on the jacket, Marius saw, to his amazement, that it was some kind of uniform, and he had also seen that Jan was armed with a pistol. That meant he was either a German or some sort of Norwegian Nazi, or else someone so actively anti-German that his presence in the house was like dynamite. Whether Jan was going to live or die, Marius simply had to know who he was: everything he did to try to save him, or even to dispose of his body if he failed, would depend on that answer. He asked him where he came from, and when he bent down to hear what Jan was trying to say, he heard the name Overgaard, which is a place at the head of the fjord. He knew that was a lie, because he had seen Jan's tracks and they came from the opposite direction; and the fact that he tried to tell a lie was reassuring, because a Nazi would be too powerful to have any need to do so.

Marius had heard about Toftefjord and suspected the truth already. He sent the women out of the room, and when they had shut the door he said, "Listen to me. If you're a good man, you've come among good people. Now, speak out." Jan told him then, in a halting whisper. Marius heard him out, and took his resolve at once. "Don't worry," he said, "we'll look after you. Go to sleep." Jan asked him what his name was, and he told him Hans Jensen, which is the same as to say John Jones. He asked where he was, and this Marius told him truthfully: in the hamlet of Furuflaten, where the valley of Lyngdalen reaches Lyngenfjord. In the three days since the avalanche, all Jan's wanderings had carried him seven miles. Marius also told him that it was the 8th of April, late in the afternoon.

When he was satisfied that he had got the truth, Marius called his sisters in again and told it to them in whispers. They went to work again, looking at Jan with new pity at what they had heard, but with a desperate anxiety for themselves and the children. Nobody whatever must hear of it, Marius had said; and they could hear him saying the same thing, again and again, to the boys.

He came back to the bed when he had made sure that the children understood him, and looked down at the ghastly face on the pillow. He was trying to think ahead. He was also beginning to see the explanation of some strange events which had happened since the storm. The Germans had suddenly searched every house in Furuflaten. They had been through his own house and his sister's from top to bottom. They were looking for radio sets, they had said; but everyone had thought at the time there was something more behind it, because the place had been searched thoroughly enough for radio sets before. And for the first time, in the last few days, there had been motorboats patrolling on the fjord, which did not fit in with the radio story. Now, Marius knew what they were searching for. There was the object of all the activity, lying at his mercy on his sister's children's bed.

Jan's luck was still good when it took him to that

door. Marius Grönvold was a very unusual man. He
was in his early thirties then, still a bachelor, a short
strong stocky man with the face of a peasant and an
extraordinarily alert and well-stocked mind. His occupation in those days was typical of this contrast: he
ran a small farm, and also wrote for the Tromsö paper.
His hobbies were politics and Norwegian literature. He
knew the Norwegian classics well, and could recite in
verse or prose for hours together, and often did so to
entertain himself or anyone else who would listen; and
he was already a leading member of the local Liberal
party, and well on his way to becoming the most prominent citizen in those parts: the sort of man, one might
say, who was destined from birth to become a mayor
or the chairman of the county council. With these politics and his love of Norwegian history and culture, it
went without saying that he was a member of the local
resistance group in Lyngenfjord, which was a branch of
the one in Tromsö.

To speak of a resistance movement in a place like
Lyngenfjord might be a little misleading. There was an
organization, but there was hardly anything it could
do. There had never been time when Norway was invaded to call up or train the people in those far-off
northern areas. The battle had been fought and lost before they had had a chance to go and take part in it.
Ever since then, they had been entirely cut off from the
world outside the German orbit. Their radio sets had
been confiscated, and the papers they read were cen-
sored by the Germans. All that they ever heard of the
fight that was going on from England was in occasional whispered scraps of clandestine news passed on
from mouth to mouth from somebody who had hidden
a radio somewhere or seen a copy of an illegal newspaper. Yet men like Marius resented their country's
enslavement as deeply as anyone: even more strongly
perhaps because they had not done anything themselves to try to stop it. It lay heavily on their con-
sciences that they had not been soldiers when soldiers
were needed so badly, and that brave deeds were still
being done while they could not find any way to test

their own bravery. Their organization was really a kind of patriotic club. None of its members had any military knowledge; but at least they could talk freely among themselves, and so keep up each other's resolution, and help each other not to sink into the belief that the Germans could win the war and the occupation go on for ever; and they knew they could count on each other for material help as well if it was ever needed.

This was the background of Marius's thoughts while he worked on Jan's feet and fed him and kept him warm. The problem which Jan had brought with him was not a mere matter of a night in hiding and a little food. Probably Jan still thought, if he thought at all, that after a good sleep he would get up and walk away; but anyone else who saw him could tell he would be an invalid for weeks, and that walking was the last thing he would do. Marius, turning things over in his mind, could see no end to the problem in front of him, except capture. Furuflaten was a tiny compact community of a few hundred people; and it was on the main road and convoys of German lorries passed through it day and night, and it had a platoon of Germans quartered in its school. He could see the German sentries on the road when he looked out of his sister's window. He could not think how he could keep Jan's presence secret. Even to buy him a little extra food would be almost impossible. Much less could he see how he could ever nurse him back to fitness and start him off on his journey again. But there was never the slightest doubt in his mind that he was going to try: because this was his challenge; at last it was something which he and only he could possibly do. If he could never do anything else to help in the war, he would have this to look back on now; and he meant to look back on it with satisfaction, and not with shame. He thanked God for sending him this chance to prove his courage.

Jan was restless and nervous. He kept dozing off into the sleep which he needed so badly, but as soon as he began to relax, he roused himself anxiously. It was a symptom of his feeble mental state. He felt terribly defenseless, because he could not see. He was afraid of being betrayed; but if he had been in his right mind and able to see Marius's honest worried face, he would have trusted him without the slightest qualm.

Marius, in fact, was watching over him with something very much like affection: the feeling one has toward any helpless creature which turns to one for protection. He had already promised his protection in his own mind, and in the best words he could think of, and it upset him that he had not succeeded in putting Jan's fears to rest. He wanted to find some way to soothe him and make him believe in his friendship; and on an impulse, when the women were not listening, he took hold of Jan's hand and said very emphatically and clearly, "If I live, you will live, and if they kill you I will have died to protect you." Jan did not answer this solemn promise, but its sincerity had its effect. He relaxed then, and fell asleep.

He slept so deeply that even the massaging of his hands and legs did not disturb him. His legs were the worst. Marius and his sisters worked on them in turns for the whole of that night and the following day, trying to get the blood to circulate. Quite early, they invented a simple test to see how far up they were frozen. They pricked them with needles, starting at the ankles and working upward. When they began, the legs were insensitive up to the knees. Above that, the needle made them twitch, although even this treatment did not disturb Jan's sleep. But as they rubbed the legs, hour by hour, they came back to life, inch after inch, and showed a reaction lower and lower down. Jan did not wake at all during the first night and day after he came in. When he did, even his feet were alive, and he woke with a searing pain where they had been numb before. Hanna Pedersen gave him a little food, and then he went to sleep again.

Although their efforts seemed to be succeeding, Marius and his sisters were all afraid that there might be some better treatment for frostbite which they had never heard of; and so it happened that the first time

Marius invoked the organization was to ask for a doctor's advice. He went first of all to Lyngseidet: a
journey of twenty minutes by bus, which covered the
whole of the distance which had taken Jan four days.
His object there was to talk to the headmaster of the
state secondary school, whose name was Legland. There
were two reasons for seeing him: one was that he was
the member of the organization who had direct contact
with the leadership in Tromsö; and the other was that
most of the people of Lyngenfjord were in the habit of
going to him when they were perplexed or in trouble.
Herr Legland was a patriarch, revered by all his neighbors. The more intelligent of them, in fact, had all been
his pupils, for he was an old man by then, and his
school served the whole of the district. It was from him
that Marius had learned his love of literature as a boy,
and he regarded him as the wisest man he knew. Besides, he was a patriot of the old uncompromising
school of Björnson and Ibsen. To him, the invasion of
Norway was a barbarous affront, a new dark age. His
school buildings in Lyngseidet had been requisitioned as
a billet for German troops: a symbol of the swamping
of the nation's culture by the demands of tyranny.

When Marius sought out this shrewd old gentleman
and told him his story, he gave his approval of what
Marius and his family had done, and he agreed with
what he proposed to do. It went without saying that he
would give his help. At the bottom of all the ideas
which Marius had thought of up to then was the
difficulty, and the necessity, of keeping Jan's presence
secret from the people of Furuflaten. It was not that
there was anyone really untrustworthy there; but there
were plenty of gossips. As soon as it leaked out at all,
the whole village would know about it as fast as exciting news can travel; and then it would only be a
matter of time before the Germans found out about
it too. Nobody would tell them; but living right in the
center of the place, in the school, they had a good idea
of what went on there. They only had to keep their eyes
open; it was a most difficult place for keeping secrets.

The houses are widely spaced on each side of the river
which runs out of Lyngdalen, and along the road
which runs close beside the shore. There are hardly
any trees, and from the middle one can see almost
every house and most of the ground between them. It
would only need a few too many neighbors calling at
Marius's house, out of curiosity or with offers of help,
for the Germans on watch at the school, or patrolling
the road, to notice that something unusual was happening.

From this point of view, to get a doctor to come
and look at Jan would be very risky. Marius's house
was the farthest up the valley, and the farthest away
from the road. The doctor would have to leave his car
on the road and go on skis for half a mile, all among
the houses; and of course as soon as he had gone,
they would have everyone up there kindly inquiring
who was ill. If the worst came to the worst, they would
have to try it; but at present all they needed was advice
and some medicine, if there was any medicine that was
any good.

This meant sending a message to Tromsö. If they
asked the local doctor, or got a prescription made up at
the local dispensary, they would have to say whom it
was for, and have two or three outsiders in on the
secret; but in Tromsö inquiries like that could be made
without anyone knowing exactly where they came
from.

Luckily, the road to Tromsö was still open,
though as soon as the spring thaw set in it would become impassable for two or three weeks. To send a private car would be difficult, because the driver would
have to give a good reason for his journey at every
roadblock he came to; but people had noticed that the
Germans never bothered much about a bus. If it was
one which ran a regular service on the road, so that they
knew it by sight, they usually let it through without
questioning the driver. One of the local bus drivers
was a member of the organization. Marius and Legland
asked him to do the job and he agreed. One of the

bus company's buses was put out of action, and the driver set off in another to fetch a spare part to repair it.

The arrival of this man in Tromsö was the first indication the leaders had had that there was any survivor from Toftefjord. Legland sent the driver to Sverre Larsen, the newspaper editor, whose right-hand man Knudsen had been deported. Naturally, his message was only verbal. Larsen did not know the driver, and the organization was still more than usually wary and on edge. Larsen refused to commit himself, and told the driver he could come back later in the day. But as soon as he had gone, he set about checking the man's credentials through the organization's chain of command; and by the time he came back he had made sure that he was not a German agent, which he very well might have been, and had already consulted a doctor and a chemist about frostbite. Both of them said there was nothing to be done which had not been done already except to alleviate the pain, and the chemist had made up a sedative. Jan got the first dose of it that evening.

In the meantime, Marius had moved Jan from his sister's house and hidden him in a corner of his barn. He knew it would not make any difference where he put him if the Germans came up to his farm to search, but at least the barn was safer from casual visitors and family friends. These were a constant worry. Jan had come to the house on a Saturday. On a fine Sunday in spring the people of Furuflaten are in the habit of skiing a little way up the valley by way of a constitutional; and that Sunday the valley was full of Jan's tracks, which led in the end, plainly enough for anyone to see, up to Hanna Pedersen's door. For anyone to go about on foot was unheard of, and foot tracks instead of ski tracks were the very thing to set people talking. To forestall inquiries, Marius went out and inspected his farm early that Sunday morning, leaving his skis at home, and mixed up his own footsteps with Jan's. He thought out some story to explain why he had done such an eccentric thing. It was a thin story, but good enough to put people off the idea that the tracks had been made by a stranger. They would merely think that the man of the house had taken leave of his senses.

At that stage, the Grönvold family were the only people in Furuflaten who were in the know: Marius, his three sisters and the two small boys, and Marius's mother. Hanna's husband was away at the fishing, and Marius had the added worry of having no other man in the family to talk to. His sisters never relaxed their efforts to nurse Jan back to health; but women in the far north are not often consulted by men in matters of opinion, and Marius could not help being aware that Jan's sudden arrival had been a serious shock to them all. His mother, in particular, was far from strong, and he was seriously troubled by the strain which it put on her. In fact, it must be a terrible thing for an elderly woman to know that her family is deeply involved in something which carries the death penalty for them all if they are caught. At one moment near the beginning she was inclined to oppose the whole thing, though of course she had no clear idea of the only alternative; but Jan had told Marius by then about his father and sister in Oslo, and Marius put it to her from Jan's father's point of view. "Suppose I was in trouble down in Oslo," he said, "and you heard that the people there refused to help me." In these simple terms she could see the problem better. It made her think of Jan as a human being, a Norwegian boy very much like her own, and not just as a stranger from a war which she had never quite understood. She gave Marius her consent and blessing in the end. Yet it is doubtful whether she ever quite recovered from the nervous tension of the years after Jan arrived there: for the strain did not end when Jan finally went away. Till the very end of the war the risk remained that some evil chance would lead the Germans to discover what she and her children had done. In the upside-down world of the occupation, the Pharisee was rewarded, and the good Samaritan was a criminal. People who acted in accordance with the sim-

plest of Christian ethics were condemned to the life
of fear which is only normally lived by an undiscovered
murderer.

The two boys were a further worry. To send them
to school every day when they knew what they did
was a heavy responsibility to put upon children. Some
children often can play a secretive role in a matter of
life and death as well as anyone older; but to go on
doing it for long will wear them down.

Jan lay for nearly a week in the barn. For four
days he was never more than semi-conscious; and that
was just as well, because he could not have moved in
any case, and when he did rise out of his drugged sleep
the pain of his feet and hands and his blinded eyes was
bad. But he was certainly getting better. Toward the
end of the week his eyesight was coming back. He began to see the light of the barn door when it was
opened, and then to recognize the faces of the people
who came to feed him. By that time, also, it looked as
if his feet would recover in the end, though he was still
a long way from being able to stand on them or walk.
Most important of all, his brain had got over the concussion, and his power of thought and his sense of
humor had come back: he was himself again. He and
Marius began to find they had a lot in common. Their
experience and background could hardly have been
more different within a single nation: one the arctic
farmer and country-bred philosopher, the other the
town technician; one cut off from the war, the other entirely immersed in military training. But Jan's sense of
comedy was never far away, and Marius, though he
was a serious-minded man, was irrepressible when he
was amused. He listened to Jan's stories of England
and the war with the greed of a starving man who has
an unexpected feast spread out in front of him, and
when Jan told him about the many ridiculous aspects
of army life, it made him laugh. When Marius laughed,
it was as if he would never stop. It was an odd infec-
tious falsetto laugh which started Jan laughing too; and
then Marius, squatting beside him in the hay in the

darkened barn, would rock with renewed merriment
and wipe away the tears which poured down his cheeks,
and they had to remind each other to be quiet, in case
anyone heard the noise outside.

But although there were these moments when
Marius enjoyed Jan's company, he remained a most
serious danger as long as he stayed on the farm. There
was an alarm every time someone was sighted climbing
the hill from the village, and every time the Germans
in the schoolhouse made some slightly unusual move.
He had to be taken away from there as soon as he was
fit enough to go, and Marius had thought of a place
to put him.

The opposite shore of Lyngenfjord is steep and
uninhabited. There had once been a farm over there:
just one in a stretch of eight miles. But it had been
burned down a long time before, and had never been
rebuilt. One small log cabin had escaped the fire and
was still standing. It was four miles from the nearest
house, either along the shore or across the water, and so
far as Marius knew, nobody ever went there. If any
safe place could be found for Jan, that seemed the most
likely. The name of the farm had been Revdal.

To get Jan across there was more than Marius
could manage with only the help of his sisters, because
he would have to be carried all the way down to a boat
and out of it again at the other side; and so at this stage
he began to bring in other members of the organization
from the village. He chose them on the principle that no
two men from one family should be mixed up in the
affair, in case something happened and another family
besides his own was entirely broken up. In the end, he
let three of his friends into his secret: Alvin Larsen,
Amandus Lillevoll and Olaf Lanes. All of them had
known one another since they were children. When he
told them about it, one by one, they all offered eagerly
to help.

They agreed to make the move on the night of the
12th of April. In the fortnight since Toftefjord, the
nights had got quite a lot shorter: uncomfortably short
for anything illegal. To avoid disaster, the first part of

the journey would have to be planned with care and carried out without the least delay. This was the half-mile from Marius's barn to the shore.

Marius had lived there all his life, but it was a new experience for him, as it would be for most law-abiding people, to plan a way out of his own home which he could use without being seen. It was extraordinarily difficult. Jan would have to be carried on a stretcher, and the two sides of the valley set limits to the routes which could be used, because they were both too steep to climb. On the other hand, the triangle of gently sloping ground between them was in full view of the houses, and the paths which crossed it led from door to door. There were two principal dangers, the German garrison in the school and the sentry who patrolled the road. But what worried Marius almost more than these was the thought of meeting a series of neighbors and having to stop to give endless explanations. To carry a man on a stretcher through one's village in secret at dead of night is a thing one cannot explain away in a casual word or two.

Marius made a reconnaissance, looking at his home from this unfamiliar point of view. There turned out to be only one possible route, and that was the river bed. The river, which is called Lyngdalselven after the valley, runs down through the middle of the village and under the road by a bridge about two hundred yards from the shore. It has a double channel, one about fifty feet wide which carries the normal summer flow, and another much wider flood channel which only fills up during the thaw in spring. That mid-April, the thaw had not yet begun, and the whole of the river was still frozen. The flood channel has banks about fifteen feet high, and Marius found that close below them, on the dry bed of the river, one was fairly well hidden from view. There was one snag about it. The nearest of all the houses to the channel was the schoolhouse where the Germans lived. It stands within three or four paces of the top of the bank. But even so, it still seemed that this was the only way. Looking out of the schoolhouse windows the troops could see almost

every inch of the valley mouth. The only place they
could not see was the foot of the bank immediately
below their windows.

When dusk began on the night which they had
chosen, they all assembled in the barn. Two men
were to go with Marius and the stretcher. His sister
Ingeborg had volunteered to go ahead of it to see that
the way was clear. Another man was to climb to the
top of a high moraine on the other side of the river,
where he could watch the sentry on the road. A rowboat with a sail had already been hauled up on the
beach at the river mouth. Jan had been wrapped in
blankets and tied to a homemade stretcher, and they
had a rucksack full of food and a paraffin cooker to
leave with him in Revdal. They waited nervously for
the long twilight to deepen till it was dark enough to
go. It was after eleven when Marius gave the word.

It was a breathless journey. For once, they could
not use their skis. To ski with a stretcher down steep
slopes among bushes in the dark could only end in
disaster, at least for the man on the stretcher. But to
carry his weight on foot in the deep snow was exhausting work, even for such a short distance. They started
by climbing straight down to the river, and when they
got to the bottom of the bank without any alarm they
put Jan down in the snow for a few minutes and rested.
The lookout left them to cross the river and go up to
his vantage point, and Ingeborg went ahead to see what
was happening at the school, and to tread out a path
in the snow. It was very quiet, but there was a light
southerly breeze which hummed in the telephone wires
and stirred the bare twigs of the bushes; it was not
much, but it helped to cover the sound of their movements. When they had got their breath they bent down
and picked up the stretcher and set off down the channel toward the school.

It soon came in sight. There were lights in some
of the windows which cast yellowish beams on the trod-
den snow outside it. One of them shone out across the
river channel, but close in, right under the wall of the
building, the steep bank cast a shadow which looked

like a tunnel of darkness. The stretcher bearers approached it, crouching as low as they could with their burden, keeping their eyes on Ingeborg's footsteps in front of them in case they should stumble, and resisting the impulse to look up at the lights above them. When they came to the fence of the playground, they crept closer in under the bank. In an upward glance they could see the edge of the roof on their right, and the beam of light lit up some little bushes on their left, but it passed a foot or two over the tops of their heads. The troops in the school were not making a sound, and the men were acutely conscious of the faint squeak and crunch of the snow beneath their tread. The silence seemed sinister. It made the thought of an ambush come into their minds. But in thirty seconds they passed the school: and there was the road, fifty paces ahead of them.

This was the place they had feared. With the school behind them and the road ahead, there was nowhere for four men to hide themselves. It all depended on luck: how long they would have to wait for the sentry, and whether a car came past with headlights. But Ingeborg was there, behind a bush at the side of the road, where she had been lying to watch the sentry, and she came back toward them and pointed to the right, away from the river bridge. That was the way they wanted the sentry to go, the longest leg of his beat. At the same moment, there was a tiny spark of light on the top of the moraine; the watcher there had struck a match, and that was the signal that the sentry was nearly at the far end of the beat and would soon be turning around. It was now or never: they had to go on without a pause. They scrambled up onto the road. For a few seconds they were visible, dark shadows against the snow, from the school and the whole of the beat and a score of houses. Then they were down on the other side, among bushes which gave them cover as far as the shore. The worst of the journey was over.

When they had hauled the boat down the beach and bundled Jan on board it, they rowed off quietly for a couple of hundred yards, and then set the lugsail and got under way, with the breeze on the starboard beam and a course toward the distant loom of the mountains across the fjord, under which was the cabin of Revdal.

9

The Deserted Farm

What Jan came to know as the Savoy Hotel, Revdal, was not very commodious, but the first two days he spent there were the happiest and most peaceful of the whole of his journey, a short fool's paradise: if one can use the word happy about his state of mind, or the word paradise about a place like Revdal. The hut was

ten feet long and seven feet wide, and you could stand upright under the ridge of the roof. It was built of logs, and it had a door but no window. The only light inside it when the door was shut came through chinks in the

wall and the roof, which was covered with growing
turf. On one side, it had a wooden bunk, and the rest
of the space in it was filled with odds and ends which
seemed to have been salvaged, long before, from the
ruins of the burned-out farm. There was a small, roughly hewn table, and some pieces of a wooden plough,
and some other wooden instruments which Jan could
not imagine any use for, and an elaborate carved picture frame without any glass or picture. Everything was
made of wood, unpainted, even the latch and hinges on
the door, and it was all worn with years of use, and
white and brittle with age.

As they carried him up there from the boat, he had
had a glimpse of its surroundings. It stands about ten
yards back from the shore, in a small clearing which
slopes up to the forest of little twisted trees which
clings to the side of the mountain. He had seen posts
and wires in the clearing, which looked as if someone
still came there to cut and dry the crop of hay, which
is a precious harvest in the north. But there was no sign
that anyone had been there for the past eight months
of winter, and it was very unlikely that anyone would
come for another three months, until July. Under the
towering masses of snow and rock the solitary deserted
little hut looked insignificant and forlorn, and even
smaller than it really was. From a distance one would
have taken it for a boulder, three-quarters covered by
snow. There was no landing place to draw attention
to it, only the lonely beach. A stranger might have
sailed along the fjord ten times and never seen it.

They put Jan in the bunk, and put the food and
the paraffin stove on the table within his reach. Marius hesitated a little while, as if there should have been
something else he could do for Jan, but there was nothing. He promised to come back two or three nights later
to see him, and Jan thanked him, and then he went out
and shut the door and left Jan alone there in the dark.
For a few minutes Jan listened, hoping to hear the
crunch of the boat on the beach as they pushed it off;
but inside the hut it was absolutely silent. When he
was sure they had gone away, he spread out his

meager belongings around him, and settled down on the hard boards of the ancient bunk. He was as contented as he could be. He had everything he wanted: time, and a little food, and solitude. He could lie there as long as he liked, not much of a burden to anyone, until his feet got all right again. Very soon he drifted off to sleep.

He had had a capacity for sleep, ever since the avalanche, which seemed to have no limit, and there was nothing to wake for in Revdal except to eat. Sometimes when hunger did wake him there was daylight shining through the holes in the roof: sometimes there was not, and he groped for his matches and ate by the dim blue gleam of the paraffin cooker. But whether it was day or night outside no longer had any interest for him.

When he was awake, he daydreamed, about Oslo before the war, his family, his football club at home where he had been president, the adventures which he had packed into the three years since he left home, and about his friends in the training camp in Scotland, and about his own ambitions and hopes for the time when the war was over. It had been a long journey and a very strange one all the way from his home and his father's instrument makers' workshop to this bunk and this hut and this desolate arctic shore; but he never thought then that it would end there. Some time, he would get up and go out of the door and begin all over again. And meanwhile, time was passing, and that was all that mattered; because time, he believed, was the only thing which could cure his feet and give him the strength to tackle the last twenty-five miles to Sweden.

But Marius, back in Furuflaten, was not so optimistic. He felt troubled in his mind at having left Jan all alone: he would much rather have hidden him somewhere where he could have kept an eye on him day and night. But he consoled himself by thinking that he had done it more for his family's sake than for his own, and also that it was in Jan's own interest to be in a place which the Germans were very unlikely to search. He believed, just as Jan did, that in time he would be fit again, but he thought it might be a very long time; and he knew, although Jan did not, how difficult it was going to be to keep him supplied with even the barest necessities of life across at Revdal. He would never have grudged him anything, neither time nor danger, nor money while his savings lasted out; but he was very much afraid that keeping things secret, which was so difficult already, would become impossible if it had to go on very long. If people noticed him going off two or three nights a week in a boat toward the uninhabited side of the fjord, there was no credible explanation he could give; and besides, there was always the chance that the Germans might yet make some sudden swoop which would prevent him from crossing at all. They might come and arrest him, and in case they did, he would have to find somebody who could not be connected with the affair but who could take over his responsibilities when he was gone. Otherwise, Jan would be left there till he starved. What it came to, in fact, was that there might be a crisis at any time; and therefore there ought to be a plan to get Jan over the frontier if the crisis came before he could go on his own feet.

Marius went to Herr Legland again, and they had a long discussion. They agreed that apart from being safer in Revdal, Jan was better placed there for an attempt on the frontier. If he had tried to go straight from Furuflaten, there would have been valleys to cross, and the main road; but from Revdal one only had to climb straight up for 3000 feet and one was right on the plateau. Once one was up there, there was no road or habitation whatever before the frontier, and the skiing was straightforward. But if Jan needed help on the journey, it would have to come from one of the settlements on the other side of the fjord.

Marius may have felt disappointed at the idea that he might have to hand Jan over to somebody else, but he had to agree that if it came to a dash for the frontier, he could not be of any help. For one thing, he had never been up on the plateau; and besides, there was no knowing how long the journey might take. It would certainly not be less than four days, and if he was away from home for as long as that, everybody would know it. But on the other hand, there was at least one settlement on the other side where there was no German garrison at all. The men from there would know the plateau, or at least the part of it near at hand, and it would be much easier for them to disappear for a few days.

When Marius had reluctantly agreed with this conclusion, Herr Legland undertook to send a warning to people he knew on the other side that an escort might be needed for the frontier. He meant to arrange a meeting place and a code word for the operation in case it had to be undertaken in a hurry.

The name of the settlement they had in mind is Mandal. It lies in a deep valley which penetrates for twenty miles into the plateau, and it has a population of six or seven hundred. It is much more cut off from the world than Lyngseidet or Furuflaten. There is no road to it, and not a single pass through the mountains to give access to it by land. It can only be reached by climbs which are always dangerous in winter, or else by a sea voyage of ten miles from Lyngseidet. But even there the organization had its contacts.

As soon as they began to think about Mandal, it brought them up against a problem which had already been causing both of them some worry, the problem of money. If Mandal had to come into it, the whole business of rescuing Jan was going to cost more than Herr Legland or Marius could possibly find out of their own pockets or their neighbors'. One is apt to forget that this sort of activity needs money, but it does: or at least, it did in north Norway. People like Marius were glad to stretch their own rations to feed Jan, and to sleep with a blanket less on their own beds, and to give him their clothes; but sooner or later he was sure to need something which neither of them possessed themselves. Then there would be only one option: either to go to somebody who could supply it, and let him into the secret so that he would give it for nothing, or else to buy it. The things Jan was most likely to need, the simple necessities of life, were rationed, and a lot of things he might possibly need could not be bought at all except at black market prices; and of course a man who was willing to sell on the black market was the last sort of person one would want to know about Jan. The only safe way to get what was needed would be to pay the price which was asked, however high it was, and not tell anybody. Jan had already had the last of all the brandy and cigarettes that Marius could lay his hands on, and he needed more; or to be accurate, he needed brandy, to keep him going in the cold, and cigarettes were the only luxury he could enjoy. If Mandal came into it too, there was going to be the question of diesel oil for boats. There was a telephone in Mandal, but all telephones were tapped. The only way to tell the Mandal men what was happening would be to get a motorboat and go there, and if the owner of the boat could not give a proper reason for the journey, the fuel would have to come from the black market too.

There was also the question of paying people for the time they spent on a job of this kind. Marius was his own master and could afford to take time off to look after Jan, and so could the other Furuflaten people. But a lot of men around there, especially in a place like Mandal, lived from hand to mouth, and if they lost a few days' work it really meant less to eat for their wives and children. That might not prevent them from helping, but the organization's principle was that nobody ought to suffer real financial hardship for anything he was asked to do. The state paid its soldiers, and the organization expected to do the same. Certainly if anyone had to be asked to take Jan across to Sweden, he would have to have his income made up for the days he was away. One way or another, the whole operation might cost much more than the resources of Lyngseidet and Furuflaten could afford.

Luckily, Herr Legland had to go into Tromsö, and he promised Marius he would take care of this question of finance. Thus for the second time news reached the city of what was happening in Lyngenfjord. Legland went to Sverre Larsen, whose father, the dismissed owner of the newspaper, was an old friend of his. He arrived on a Saturday evening, and told Larsen the whole story from beginning to end, except that he left out all the names of people and places. He had reckoned that he must have a fund of £150 for urgent expenses which he could already foresee. Without it, or the certainty of being able to get it quickly, he would not feel he could ask anyone to go to the frontier.

Larsen accepted the request without any question. It was the kind of thing which the Tromsö merchants expected to pay for. But it was a stern test of his organization to find the money in cash on a Saturday night. If Legland had come at a time when the banks and offices were open, it would only have taken a few minutes. As it was, Larsen himself put in all the money which he happened to have in the house, and then went the rounds of his friends in the organization. By Sunday morning he had collected it all, in varying sums from a lot of different people, and Herr Legland took it home, with his money worries set at rest for the time being. But as things turned out, this was only the very beginning of the expense of saving Jan's life. Before the end, it cost £1,650 in cash, besides the labor and goods which were given freely by hundreds of people; and the whole of this sum was contributed by business houses and individuals in Tromsö who regarded him as a symbol of the battle against the Germans.

Marius kept his promise to go back and visit Jan. Two nights after he had left him at Revdal, he set off again and rowed across the fjord, taking a new stock of food and some bottles of milk. Jan was still in the bunk, exactly as he had left him. He was cheerful, and the rest was doing him good. He had been amusing himself by pulling out the moss which had been used to caulk the joints between the logs of the wall of the hut, and rolling it in newspaper to make cigarettes. Marius swore that before next time he would find something better to smoke than that. Meanwhile, he cooked up some fish for him, and when he had eaten it they both had a look at his feet. They seemed to be getting on all right, and they talked things over in the hope that Jan would be able to put on skis again before very long.

They had already agreed that Jan ought not to know anything about the organization. Although his prospects looked a little brighter than they had a week before, both he and Marius knew in their heart of hearts that so long as he could not walk his chance of avoiding being captured in the end was really very small. So Marius still called himself Hans Jensen, and Jan did not know any names at all for the other people he had seen, or anything about the activities in Lyngseidet or Tromsö. He had to be content not to know who was helping him, but just to be grateful for the help when it arrived.

However, Marius did tell him that night, in order to keep his spirits up, that people in Mandal were being asked to stand by in case their help was needed; and he explained the geography of the surrounding mountains and the plateau, so that Jan would have it clear in his head if they had to take sudden action. It is not very far across the mountains from the hut at Revdal into the valley of Mandal: only about five miles on the map, though it involves the climb of 3000 feet up to the plateau level and down again. If Jan needed help when the time came, Marius meant to come to Revdal and lead him up the climb; and he would arrange for the Mandal men to come up from the other side and meet them on top, so that they could take over there and escort Jan southward across the plateau till he came to the frontier.

It was encouraging for Jan to know that some positive plans had been made to get him away, and Marius left him that night in good humor, and quite contentedly resigned to another two days of solitude and darkness.

It was soon after Marius left, not more than a few hours, that Jan's feet began to hurt. It was nothing much at first, only a slight increase in the pain which had been going on ever since they were thawed. It came and went, and sometimes, that early morning, he thought it was imagination. But by the time when sunlight began to come through the holes in the roof, he was sure that something was happening. He struggled out of his blankets, when it was as light as it ever got in the hut, and unwrapped his feet. The sight of them alarmed him. They had changed visibly since the night before when Marius was with him. Now, his toes seemed to be gray, and although his feet as a whole were more painful than they had been, the ends of his toes were numb and cold, as if he had pins and needles. He rubbed them, but it only made them hurt more, and the skin began to peel off them. The toe which had been wounded had begun to heal, but the scar had a dark unhealthy look.

He rolled himself up again in the blankets and lay there uneasily, wondering what it meant. He did not know what had gone wrong, or what he ought to do to try to stop it. For the first time since he had met Marius, he began to feel lonely. It had seemed so easy to say he would wait for another two days alone, but now he regretted it. He wanted very much to have someone to talk to about his feet. He knew that the thirty-six hours he still had to wait before he could hope to see Marius were going to pass very slowly.

They turned out to be infinitely worse than he expected. The pain grew with appalling quickness, hour by hour. It grew so that sleep became out of the question and he could only lie there staring into the darkness and counting every minute till Marius might arrive, moving his legs in hopeless attempts to find a position which would ease them. The pain spread up his legs in waves, and sometimes seemed to fill his whole body like a flame so that when it receded it left him sweating and trembling and breathless.

In the second dawn, when the light was strong enough, he unwrapped his feet again. After the night he had just survived, what he saw then did not surprise him. His toes were black and swollen, and a foul-smelling fluid was oozing out of them, and he could not move them at all anymore.

He was shocked and bewildered, with nobody to
appeal to for advice or comfort. When the pain was
at its worst, he could hardly think at all. When it eased,
he lay there, wondering what Marius would do: whether
he would take him back to Furuflaten, or whether
there was any doctor who would take the risk of coming
to Revdal. He wondered whether there was anything that even a doctor could do, without taking him to
hospital. He thought he had either got blood poisoning
or gangrene. Either of them, he imagined, would spread
farther and farther up his legs. If he had been in hospital, he thought, they would have given him injec-
tions and stopped it before it got too far; but there in
Revdal, without any kind of medical equipment, he
could not think of anything to do. He wondered whether he ought to agree to go to hospital if he got the
chance, and soon made up his mind that he should not.
In hospital, the Germans would certainly get him in
the end, and all kinds of people might get themselves
into trouble on his behalf. He knew it might be
tempting to agree if the pain went on, so he took a firm
and final decision there and then, in case he was not
in a fit condition to decide when the moment came;
he would not go to hospital whatever happened. He
tried to think of the worst that could possibly happen,
so that this resolve would never weaken, and after all,
the worst was only death. He put all his faith in Marius.
Marius would know what to do: he would either
take him to a doctor or bring a doctor to Revdal; or if
he could not do either of those things, he would get
advice and borrow medicine and come and doctor
him himself. This thought kept him going all through
the second day.

At long last the evening came. The little shafts of
light inside the hut began to fade, and the darkness
he had longed for all day set in. Marius could not begin to row across till it was dark, so that an hour and a
half of night must pass before he could be expected.
But long before that, Jan lay and listened for the footsteps outside the door, and the cheerful greetings which
Marius always gave him before he came in, so that he

would know it was a friend who was coming. The minutes of the night dragged on and on till the first light of the dawn, and Marius did not come.

A period of time began then which Jan remembered, after it ended, with the utmost horror. It was the first time that he sank into absolute despair of coming through alive, and he had not really resigned himself yet to dying; at least, not to dying the lingering, lonely agonizing death which seemed to be all he could expect. At first, he waited for each night with the hope of hearing Marius; but as each night passed and nothing happened the hope slowly died within him. After five days, he could only believe that Marius and everyone who knew he was there had been arrested and shot, and that he was quite forgotten by the world, condemned to lie in the desolate hut till the poisoning killed him, or till he wasted away through starvation. Revdal, which they had chosen because it seemed safe, had turned into a trap. He was walled in by the barren mountain which hung over him, and by the sea and the miles of lonely shore on either side. He could not believe anymore that he would ever get up and go across to the door and open it and go out into the fresh air to start on his journey again. He knew his own feet would never carry him to the nearest friendly house, and he knew that so much of his strength had ebbed away that he would never be able to swim or even to crawl there.

In his loneliness, he wished he was able to pray, and lying there waiting to die he tried to set his religious beliefs in order. But like so many young men of his generation, he had grown up without the habit of saying prayers. It was not any fault of his. He had been given a technical, scientific education, and there had not been much room in it for religion. It had given him, at the age of twenty-six, a materialistic view of life. He had done his best to live in accordance with Christian ethics, but nothing he had ever been taught could help him to believe in a personal God who watched over him in Revdal. He did not despise that kind of belief, and he knew to the full what a comfort it would be to him; but nobody of a clear and serious turn of mind can change his beliefs to suit his circumstances. After living without prayers, he thought that to pray when he was in such desperate straits would be hypocritical, and an offense to any God he could believe in. Neither did he believe at that time in a future life. He believed he was already forgotten or assumed to be dead by everyone who knew him, except his father and brother and sister, and that when the last painful tenuous thread was broken he would not exist anymore, except as a rotten corpse in the bunk where he was lying.

So day followed day, each merged into another by the mists of pain. On one day, he was aware of the sound of wind, and of snow sifting through the holes in the walls and beneath the door. On another, when he put out his hand to feel for the food on the table, he found it was all gone. On all of them, when he fell into a doze, even after the last of all reasonable hope had gone, he dreamed or imagined that he could hear Marius outside the door, and he started awake with a clutch at his heart. But nobody came.

10

After the Storm

In fact, there was nothing wrong with Marius. The
Germans had not made any new move, and everything
was quiet in Furuflaten. What had stopped him coming to see Jan was simply another storm. Just after his
previous visit, it had started to blow up from the south,
and before the night when he had meant to cross the
fjord again there was such a sea running that the crossing was quite impossible.

While Jan was lying groaning in the hut on the
eastern side, Marius was fretting impatiently on the
west, and between them four miles of furious sea made
an impassable barrier. Nobody could get to Revdal. Every day, Marius watched the gray scudding water which
was streaked with spindrift, and every evening at dusk
he went down to the beach at Furuflaten to make sure
that there was really no chance of going; but it was
hopeless even to try to launch a boat. At night he lay
and listened for any easing of the shrieks of wind.

But he was not really worried. There was no reason why he should be. When he had left Jan, his health
had been improving. He had not been able to leave
as much food as he would have liked, but he reckoned
that if Jan could spin it out, there was enough to keep
him from starving for some time yet. He knew Jan
would be disappointed and would be wondering what
had happened, but he was sure that he would guess it

was the storm. He did not realize that inside the log
walls of the hut, with the snow banked up all around
them, Jan could not hear the howling of the wind.
Also, he still thought Jan was some kind of seaman and
would imagine for himself the fearsome effect of a
southerly gale in those narrow waters with a clear fetch
of twenty miles to windward.

So although Marius was naturally upset by the
feeling that he was letting Jan down, he had no immediate anxiety, and what worried him most during the
storm was the increasing menace of the daylight. So far
as his own help was still concerned, the rescue of
Jan was becoming a race against the midnight sun. It
was the beginning of the last week in April, and already it was twilight all night. While the storm lasted,
the nights were dark enough, but when the sky cleared
there would not be more than a couple of hours in
which he could sneak away from the Furuflaten beach
without being seen by the sentry; and if he left the
beach at the time when the twilight was deepest, he
would have to run the risk of landing again in
broad daylight. In a fortnight's time it would be so
light all night that anyone with binoculars would be
able to watch him the whole way across the fjord, and
if the German motorboat was still patrolling it would
be able to pick him up from miles away. Before
then, whatever happened, Jan would have to move on
from Revdal.

It was exactly a week after Marius's second visit
to the hut when the storm began to show signs of ending. During that day, when he and his family could
see that the evening might bring a chance of crossing, he
collected everything he had to offer Jan and packed it
in his rucksack: food, paraffin, bottles of milk, and a
few cigarettes. At nightfall he put on his skis and went
down to the beach again. Two of his friends were there
to meet him. There was still some sea running, but not
enough to make the passage dangerous; when the wind
drops in that landlocked water, the sea calms very
quickly. They quietly launched the boat, and began to
row away. During the storm, nothing had been seen of

the motorboat, but that made it seem all the more likely that it would be out on patrol again that night.

However, the crossing was peaceful. Marius himself was happy because he had some good news to bring to Jan. He had just heard that Herr Legland had sent a message to the schoolmaster in Mandal, and that a favorable answer had come back. There had evidently been some kind of a meeting in Mandal, and there had been plenty of volunteers who would stand by to come up to a rendezvous on top of the range between Mandal and Revdal where they would take delivery of Jan. Mandal was willing to take over the responsibility of looking after him, and the schoolmaster thought they would be able to escort him to the frontier. Marius imagined, in that brief moment of optimism while he crossed the fjord, that Jan might be in Sweden before a week had passed.

The shock when he got to Revdal was all the worse. Before he opened the door of the hut, he called "Hullo there!" But there was no answer. He went in. It was pitch dark inside, and it stank of decay. In alarm, he called Jan by his name, and stooped over the bunk as the thought flashed through his mind that the Germans had been there and taken Jan away. But he felt the bundle of blankets and then, to his relief, he heard a faint sound as Jan turned his head.

"What's the matter?" he said. "What's happened?"

"There's the hell of a pain," Jan said.

Marius hastily shut the door and lit a lantern. The sight which he saw appalled him. Jan's face was as white as the face of a corpse beneath the dirt and the straggling beard. He slowly and wearily opened his eyes when the light fell on them, and made a feeble movement. The blankets around his legs were dark with blood.

Jan was too far gone to be pleased that Marius had arrived. It had happened to him so often before in dreams. For a few moments he was even unwilling to be dragged up out of his coma and forced to make the effort to live again. But when Marius boiled some water and made him take a hot drink he revived a

little. He said that he had not had anything to eat or
drink for several days. This puzzled Marius, who
thought he had left enough; but the fact was that three
or four days before, what was left of the food had fallen
off the table, and Jan had been too bemused to realize
what had happened. Since then, he had lain there growing weak with hunger, while bread and dried fish were
lying on the floor beside him, just out of his sight below the bunk board.

When Jan had come to himself enough to be able
to talk coherently, Marius set himself to the unpleasant
job of looking at his feet. Even before he saw them,
he knew that it was gangrene. It was perfectly obvious
that although Jan was alive, the toes of both of his
feet had been dead for some time. Most of the blood
on the blankets had come from cuts which Jan had
made himself. Some days before, while he still had the
strength to do it, he had started to operate on his feet
with his pocketknife. In the belief that it might be
blood poisoning, he had reasoned that the only thing
he could do was to draw off the blood, as people used to
do with snake bites; and so he had pulled up his legs in
the bunk, one by one, and stabbed his feet with the
knife and let them bleed.

Marius washed them as best he could and bound
them up again. Both he and Jan knew, without having
to say it, that Jan would never walk or ski to Sweden.
Marius privately thought there was nothing to be done
except to amputate both feet. He did not say so to
Jan, for fear of depressing him; but Jan had also come
to the same conclusion.

Marius could not stay long that night because of
the daylight, but before he left he promised Jan that he
would either get a doctor, or else arrange somehow for
him to be carried to Sweden, and that in any case he
would come back in two or three days. Then he left him
again to his solitude. But now that Jan knew that he
still had active friends who were trying to help him,
he felt he could face another few days in that abomi-
nable hut with equanimity. The mere sight of Marius
had brought back his will to live. During the days

that followed, between the bouts of pain, he began to
come to terms with the idea of living as a cripple. At
first he dwelt morbidly on all the active pursuits which
he would lose, but by and by he began to look forward
to the simple pleasures he would still be able to enjoy. The height of his ambition at that time was to get
back to London and go into Kensington Gardens in a
wheelchair on a sunny day and watch the children playing.

Marius, rowing back across the fjord in the light
of dawn, knew he had just made promises to Jan without any idea of how he could fulfill them; but he had
great faith in the idea that if you are ready to give
up everything to the solution of any problem, you will
always find an answer. He did not know of any doctor
who he was sure would risk his life to go to Revdal,
and he did not really believe that a doctor could do
much without taking Jan to hospital, which Jan had
refused to hear of. Still less did he know, at that
moment, how Jan could be carried bodily across the
mountains to the frontier. But one or other of these
alternatives had got to be arranged, not only because
he had promised it, but also because without either
of them, Jan was obviously going to die.

As soon as he got home, he told all his friends in
the organization about the new and apparently insuper-
able difficulty that Jan was absolutely helpless. Herr
Legland and the three Furuflaten men who had carried Jan over to Revdal all discussed it with him. Bit
by bit they pieced together a not impossible plan.
Messengers were sent to Tromsö and to Mandal and to
a valley called Kaafjord even farther east. The news
of the problem spread far and wide, whispered from
one to another of the trusted people who might have
help to offer. The dormant patriotic club went into action, inspired at last by a situation which was going to
test its efficiency to the utmost. During the following
evening, the messengers began to return, one by one,
bringing criticisms and new suggestions and new offers
of help back to the main conspirators. The plan took
shape.

The man who had been to Tromsö brought back
a message from Sverre Larsen simply promising financial support, without any qualifications. The one who
had been to Mandal had a more complicated message,
but it was almost equally welcome. A party of four of
the Mandal men was ready to make the climb to the
plateau at any moment and to take the responsibility of
keeping Jan alive. If Marius and the Furuflaten
men could get Jan up there and bring a sled, they were
also willing to try to haul it to the frontier. But this
they regarded as a last resort. None of them had ever
tried to haul a sled across the plateau. It might take a
long time, and if the weather broke again it might end
in disaster. Furthermore, none of them knew the Swedish side of the mountains, and they had to point out
that although the frontier was only twenty-five miles
away, a man who did not know the country might
easily have to go another hundred miles down into the
forests toward the Baltic before he found any human
habitation. If that happened, the journey would take
so long that their absence could not possibly pass un-
noticed, and that would mean that none of them could
come back. They would have to go into exile, and this
they were most unwilling to do because all of them
had dependents. But they had a better proposal: to get
the Lapps to make the journey.

The advantage of getting Lapps to go, rather than
Norwegians, was obvious at once to Marius and Herr
Legland, as it would be to anyone who knew the Lapps
and the country. The only surprising thing was that
anyone in Kaafjord or Mandal should know any Lapps
well enough to have any hope of persuading them to
make the journey. The Lapps are very peculiar people
at any time, a small primitive race entirely distinct from
anyone else in Europe; and during the war they were
more peculiar than usual. The kind of Lapps they had
in mind are nomads who live by breeding reindeer,
and since the beginning of history they have made the
same migrations with their reindeer every year. The
same families of Lapps come every spring with their
herds to Kaafjord and Lyngseidet, always arriving

within a day or two of the fifth of May. They spend the summer there, in Norway, and the winter in Finland or Sweden. National frontiers mean nothing to them, because they have been making their journeys since long before the frontiers existed. To stop them would mean that their race would die out, because the reindeer cannot survive without a seasonal change of feeding ground, and the Lapps cannot survive without their reindeer. Probably the Germans would have liked to stop them, if only for the sake of tidiness, but they wisely never tried; and all through the World War the Lapps wandered unconcerned between Finland, which was fighting on the side of Germany, and Norway, which was fighting as best it could on the Allied side, and Sweden, which was neutral.

One result of this unique situation was that the Lapps themselves naturally had no interest in the war at all. Probably none of them had any idea of what it was all about. It was no good appealing to them on any grounds of patriotism or ideology. They were no more attached to one of the three countries than another, and they would never have heard of politics. Neither would the humanitarian grounds for helping Jan have meant very much to them, because they do not set a high value on human life. If a Lapp lost the use of his feet, like Jan, he would know he was useless and expect his family to leave him alone to die.

All the same, if any Lapps could be persuaded to take Jan to the frontier, they were much more likely to succeed than any Norwegian party could possibly be. For one thing, nobody could check their movements; there was no limit to the time they could be away. Also, although they knew nothing about compasses or maps, they knew that uncharted country far better than anyone else. They were able to survive even the worst of winter weather in the open; and finally, they had reindeer trained to draw sleds, and could cover much more ground in a day than a party of men drawing a sled themselves. Therefore Marius, Herr Legland and the rest of the conspirators welcomed this suggestion. The first wave of the migration of reindeer was due to arrive

within a week. They would already be somewhere
on their way across the mountains. The message from
Mandal had said that the best ski-runner in Kaafjord
was ready to set off, along the migration tracks toward
the Lapp settlement of Kautokeino, a hundred miles
away, to try to locate the herds. A message was sent
back, welcoming the idea and asking him to go at
once.

Meanwhile, the main problem for Marius and the
Furuflaten men was to get Jan up to the plateau. The
place for meeting the party from Mandal had already
been agreed. It was in a shallow depression on the
plateau, halfway between Revdal and Mandal. To get
there from the Revdal side was a steep climb for the
first two thousand feet, and then a more gentle upward
slope across about three miles of the open snowfield.
The meeting place itself was at a height of about 2,700
feet. Something of the nature of a stretcher which could
be carried would be needed to get him up the first
part of the climb, and a sled would be easiest for the
last part. They decided to try to combine both func-
tions by building the lightest possible sled.

All these discussions and the coming and going of
messengers had been happening in the midst of the
German garrison areas in Furuflaten and Lyngseidet.
For building the sled, the plot was carried even farther
into the German camp. The best joiner anyone could
think of was the caretaker of Herr Legland's school.
The school buildings had been requisitioned and the
pupils turned out to make room for the German district headquarters staff, but the caretaker still worked
there and still had access to what had been the school
workshop. He undertook to build the sled; and he did
so, inside the German headquarters itself. The imperti-
nence of this filled everyone who knew of it with a kind
of schoolboyish glee; and the only disadvantage of such
an attractive arrangement was that the joiner could
not take the risk of putting the sled together, because
the Germans who came in and out while he was working would have been certain to ask what it was for.
However, he made each piece to careful measurements,

and was willing to guarantee that when the time came
to assemble it, everything would fit. It was built on a
pair of ordinary skis, and it had a slatted platform about
a foot high, eighteen inches wide and six feet long.
Events proved that his workmanship was good. The
sled not only fitted together, but stood up to week after
week of the hardest possible treatment.

It was ready on the third day after Marius had
last been to Revdal, and all the plans were completed
on that day too, except that the ski-runner from Kaafjord had not come back from his search for the reindeer. Marius's three neighbors, Alvin Larsen, Olaf
Lanes and Amandus Lillevoll, were prepared to go
over with him to Revdal that night to make the attempt
to haul Jan up the mountain. Herr Legland telephoned
to the schoolmaster in Mandal to say in cautiously
chosen words, in case the line was tapped, that the parcel he was expecting was being sent at once. Alvin Larsen was going that afternoon to fetch the sled from
Lyngseidet; but that very morning an avalanche
blocked the road between Lyngseidet and Furuflaten.

Luckily, the avalanche did not delay him much,
and on the whole it was probably an advantage to their
plans. It was also the indirect cause of an incident which
appealed to what might be called the occupation sense
of humor. The local people had been expecting it to
happen. The road just north of Furuflaten runs along
the shore of the fjord below a cliff a thousand feet high,
the same cliff which Jan had been trying to skirt when
he got lost in the mountains; and the snow from the
gullies in the cliff always falls and blocks the road
about the last week in April. It happens with such reg-
ularity that a jetty has been built at Furuflaten for a
car ferry which provides a way through for traffic
till the danger is past in May. Alvin Larsen had already
arranged to go to Lyngseidet by boat if the avalanche
started before the sled was ready; but the Germans
were not so well prepared for it, and the sudden
blocking of the main road diverted their attention at
that crucial moment from everything else that was happening.

Alvin got to Lyngseidet without any trouble, and tied up his boat at the pier. There was a German sentry on the pier who took no notice of him at all. He went up to the school and collected the bits of the sled from the caretaker, together with a bag of bolts and screws, and minute instructions for putting it all to-

gether. The bundles of pieces of wood tied together with string and the pair of skis looked reasonably harmless. He carried them down through the village to the pier. But when he got there the tide was very low, and his boat was a long way down. He was afraid to throw the wood down into the boat in case it broke, and if he got down into the boat he could not reach up again to the level of the pier. So he called to the sentry to give him a hand. The sentry came over, and put down his rifle, and kindly handed the skis and the bundles down to Alvin one by one. Alvin thanked him gravely in Norwegian, and started his engine and steamed away.

11

The Ascent of Revdal

That evening, the sailing boat which Marius used crossed over the fjord again, laden with the gear for the attempt to climb the mountain: the sled, still in pieces, a sixty-foot rope, an old canvas sleeping bag and two fresh blankets for Jan, two rucksacks full of spare clothing and food and a bottle of brandy, and the four pairs of skis of the men who were making the attempt.

The ascent of Revdal was the first of two feats of mountaineering during Jan's rescue which are possibly unique. It often happens after climbing accidents in peacetime that an injured man has to be carried or lowered a long way down a mountain; but there must rarely, if ever, have been any occasion before or since to carry an injured man up a mountain for three thousand feet in severe conditions of ice and snow. At the time, spurred on by the knowledge that Jan's life depended on it, the four men who attempted it never dreamed of failure; but ever afterward, when they looked up in cold blood at the mountain wall of Revdal, they wondered how they could possibly have done it.

When they got to the far shore of the fjord that evening, they walked up to the hut in some anxiety at what they would find inside, afraid of the effect which another three days of isolation might have had on

Jan. But they found him more cheerful than he had
been the time before. Physically, he was weaker, and
those of the party who had not seen him since they had
left him there twelve days earlier were shocked at the
change in his appearance, for he had lost a lot of
weight and his eyes and cheeks were sunken. But he
was much clearer in his head than he had been when
Marius saw him, and he had even regained the vestige
of a sense of humor. He told them his feet were no
worse. The toes, of course, could not get any worse,
but the gangrene had not spread any farther, so far as
he could tell. He said it was still just as painful; but
they could see from his behavior that he could stand
up to the pain now that he knew he was not abandoned. All in all, he was a patient whom no hospital
staff would have allowed out of bed for a moment,
and looking down at him lying there in his filth, all
four men wondered whether it could be right to take
him out into the snow and subject him to the treatment they intended. All of them thought it would very
likely kill him. But they knew for certain that it was
his only chance.

     While two of them put the sled together, the
others wrapped him securely in two blankets, and
then pushed and pulled him into the sleeping bag. When
the sled was ready, they lifted him out of the bunk
where he had lain for nearly a fortnight, and put him
on the sled and lashed him securely down with ropes,
so that not much more than his eyes was showing and
he could not move at all. They maneuvered the sled
through the door and put it down in the snow outside. While they adjusted their individual loads of skis
and ski poles, and ropes and rucksacks, Jan had a moment to glance for the last time, without any regret, at
the hovel where he had expected to die. Then they took
up the short hauling ropes they had tied to the sled,
and turned it toward the mountain. It was a little after
midnight; but there was still the afterglow of the sun
in the northern sky above the mouth of the fjord,
and even beneath the mountain wall it was not very
dark. There were roughly fifteen degrees of frost.

The first part of the climb straight up from the hut at Revdal is covered by the forest of birch scrub. It is not steep enough to be called more than a scramble in mountaineering terms, but in deep snow it is the most frustrating kind of scramble, even for a climber not carrying any burden. None of the miniature trees have trunks much thicker than an arm, but they have been growing and dying there unattended since primeval times, and the ground beneath them is covered with a thick matted tangle of rotten fallen logs which gives no foothold. The trees grow very close together, and they are interlaced with half-fallen branches bowed down or broken by the weight of snow. Some trees have died and are still standing, propped up by the others crowded around them, and these break and crumble away if someone incautiously uses them for a handhold. When the deep springy mesh of fallen trees, lying piled on one another, is hidden by a smooth deceptive covering of snow, the forest is a place where a climber must go with care. It would be impossible to fall for more than a foot or two, but it would be very easy to break a leg in falling.

Getting Jan up through the forest was mostly a matter of brute strength and endless patience; but strength and patience, of course, were two of the qualities Marius had thought about when he chose his three companions. Alvin Larsen was slight and thin, and only about twenty-one years old, but he had just come back from the tough school of the Lofoten fishing and was in perfect training. Amandus Lillevoll was a little older, a small wiry man with a great reserve of strength, and an exceptional skier. Olaf Lanes was the only big man of them all. He had shoulders like an ox, and he hardly ever spoke unless he had to: the epitome of the strong silent man. As for patience, all four of them had the unending dogged patience which is typical of Arctic people.

Within the steep forest, they quickly discovered the technique which served them best. Two of them would hold the sled, belayed to a tree to stop it from running backward, while the others climbed on ahead

with the rope, forcing their way through the frozen
undergrowth. When the upper pair found a possible
stance, they took a turn of the rope around a tree and
hauled the sled up toward them, the lower pair steering
it, stopping it when it threatened to turn over, pushing
as best they could, and lifting it bodily when it buried
itself in drifts. Their progress was very slow. There was
seldom a clear enough space to haul the sled more
than about a dozen feet at a time, and each change of
stance meant a new belay and a new coiling and un-
coiling of the icy rope. The leaders, treading a trail
through the virgin snow, often fell through into holes
in the rotten wood beneath, and it was difficult to
climb out of these hidden traps. Before they had gained
more than a few hundred feet, they began to be afraid
that they had started something which it would be
impossible to finish; not so much because they thought
their own stubbornness and strength would be un-
equal to the job, but because they were more and
more afraid that Jan would not survive it. It was going
to be a long time before they got to the top; and they
had found a new problem which had no answer, and
which nobody had foreseen: the simple problem of
whether to haul him feet first or head first. When they
took him feet first, of course his head was always much
lower than his feet, and sometimes in the steep drifts he
was hanging almost vertically head downward. He
could not stand this for very long, certainly not for
hour after hour; but when they turned him around and
took him up head first, the blood ran into his feet and
burst out in new hemorrhages, and his face showed
them the pain he was trying to suffer in silence. But
as the climb went on, he was more and more often
unconscious when they looked at him. This was a mercy, but it made them all the more sure he would not
last very long. This urgency, together with the blind
faith which he seemed to have in them, made them
press on with the strength of desperation. Every few
feet of the forest brought them up against a new obstacle which had to be surmounted. They struggled
with each one till they overcame it, and then turned to

the next without daring to pause, hoping that Jan would last till they got to the top, and that then the Mandal men would be able to whisk him straight over to Sweden.

When they cleared the forest at last, at a height of about a thousand feet, they had to rest. They slewed the sled around broadside to the hill and dug in one runner so that it stood level, and collapsed in the snow beside it. Jan was awake, and they gave him a nip of brandy, and sucked some ice themselves, and looked down at the way they had come. The climb had already taken nearly three hours, and it was day. The dawn light shone on the peaks above Furuflaten across the water, and Jaeggevarre glowed above them all on the western skyline. The fjord below was still, and there was no sign of life on it. In the shadow of the hill, the air was very cold.

Immediately above the treeline was a sheer face of rock, but to their right it was broken by a steep cleft with the frozen bed of a stream in the bottom of it. Each time they had crossed the fjord they had gazed up at the face as they approached it, and the cleft had seemed the most likely route to the summit. From closer at hand, it still looked possible. To get to the bottom of it they would have to traverse a steep snow slope about two hundred feet high and perhaps a hundred yards across. The slope was clear and smooth at the top, where they would have to cross it, but at the bottom it vanished in the forest. It had a firm crust on it, and there seemed to be no particular danger about it. When they had got their breath they gathered themselves together to attempt it.

This was the first time they had tried to traverse with the sled; and crossing the slope turned out to be like a nightmare, like walking a tightrope in a dream. Three of them stood below the sled and one above it. To keep it level and stop it rolling sideways down the hill, the three men below it had to carry the outer runner, letting the inner one slide in the snow. Very slowly they edged out across the slope, kicking steps and moving one man at a time till the whole slope yawned

dizzily below them. It was impossible then to stop or
go back. The sled, resting on a single ski, moved all
too easily. While they could keep it perfectly level,
all was well, but they could feel that if they let it tilt
the least bit either way, either down by the head or
down by the foot, it would take charge and break
away from them, and then in a split second the whole
thing would be over. Kicking steps in a snow slope always demands a fair degree of balance because there
is nothing whatever to hold on to. It is impossible to
resist a sudden unexpected force. If the sled had begun
to slide they could have saved themselves by falling on
their faces and digging their hands and toes into the
snow; but they could not have stopped the sled, and
when it crashed into the trees two hundred feet below
it would have been traveling at a speed which it was
horrifying to imagine. Perhaps it was just as well that
Jan, lying on it on his back and lashed immovably
in position, could only look up at the sky and the rock
face above him, and not at the chasm down below.
Before they reached the other side of that slope, the
men were sweating and trembling with the effort and
tension. At the foot of the cleft, where the gradient
eased, they stopped again thankfully and anchored the
sled with ski poles driven into the snow, so that they
could relax till their strength came back. From there,
Jan could see the cleft soaring above them.

When they looked up at it, it seemed to be steeper
than they had expected. The walls of it were sheer,
and it was about thirty feet wide. The snow in the
bed of it showed all the signs of being about to avalanche; but it was safe enough on that western slope
just after dawn. The cleft curved gently to the left, so
that from the bottom they could not see very far up it;
but having seen it from the fjord they knew it had no
pitch in it too steep for the snow to lie on, and that it
led almost all the way to the easier slopes on the
upper half of the mountain. It was certainly going to
be difficult and it might be impossible, but now that
they had come so far there was no alternative.

After a very short rest, two of them began to lead

out the sixty-foot rope. They went up side by side, kicking two parallel sets of steps for the second pair to use. Within the cleft, they were able to use the full length of the rope for the first time, and the leaders did not pause till the whole of it was stretched up the snow above the sled. Then they dug themselves as deep a stance as they could and braced themselves in it and took the strain of the weight of the sled while the others down below them freed it from its anchors. So the first pitch of a long and heavy haul began.

In some ways, going straight up the slope was not so hard as trying to go across it. The balance of the sled was not important: it hung at the end of the rope like a pendulum. But the physical effort was greater and more sustained. At each stance the two leaders hauled the sled up toward them while the two men below followed it up the steps, pushing as best they could. At the end of each sixty feet it was anchored afresh; but the ski poles could not be trusted to hold it alone, and even the effort of holding it was so exhausting that they could not afford to pause.

Beyond the bend, the cleft swept smoothly up to a skyline appallingly far above, and there was nothing in it which offered a chance of a rest: no boulder or chockstone, and no break in the vertical walls on either side.

Somewhere in the upper reaches of the cleft, Jan came as near a sudden death as he had been anywhere on his journey. All four of the climbers by then were in that extremely unpleasant dilemma which is experienced sooner or later by every mountaineer, when one knows one has outreached one's strength, and it is too late to go down by the way one has come, so that one must either win through to the top, or fall. It was at this stage, when they knew they could never manage to lower the sled to the bottom, that what they had dreaded happened. Somebody slipped, somebody else was off balance: in a fraction of a second the sled shot backward. But Amandus happened to be below it. It hit him hard in the chest and ran over him, and somehow he and the sled became entangled together

and his body acted as a brake and stopped it, and within the second the others had it under control again. The
climb went on, and Jan did not know what had happened because he was unconscious. For the rest of the
climb and long afterward Amandus suffered from pain
in his chest, and in retrospect it seems likely that some
of his ribs were broken.

They got to the skyline; but it was not the top.
The cleft ended, and ahead of them they saw a frozen
waterfall. The ice hung down it in smooth translucent
curtains. There was no hope whatever of hauling the
sled up there. But at the bottom of it, more welcome
than anything else in the world could have been, there
was a boulder projecting through the snow, and with a
final effort they heaved the sled on top of it and wedged
it there, and were able at last to rest.

They sat down in a group around the sled, and
looked up at the next pitch. It seemed as if it might be
the last difficulty, but it looked the worst of all. The
boulder was in the middle of a little *cirque* or bowl of
rock and ice which enclosed it all around, except for
the narrow gap where their own tracks plunged down
out of sight into the cleft. This gap framed a distant
view of the fjord waters, now gleaming far below, and
the sunlit peaks beyond them. Almost all of the rim of
the bowl was as steep and inaccessible as the waterfall itself. But just to the right of the waterfall there
was one possible way of escape, up a narrow slope
which had an ice cornice at the top. The acute angle of
this slope suggested that the whole of it was ice, like the
fall, and not snow; but it was the only way out of
the bowl which was even worth attempting.

As it turned out, this was the only part of the
climb which was really rather easier than it looked.
Hard ice would have stopped the party altogether, because none of them had ice axes, and all they could use
to cut steps was the toes of their boots and the tips of
their ski poles. But when the leaders got on to the
slope, they found it was made of hard ice crystals
which could be dug away without very much trouble
and compacted firmly under their weight. They went up

it methodically, side by side as before, hacking out two
sets of steps. The slope was too long for the sixty-foot
rope, and they had to stop when they had taken out all
they could, and dig themselves in again to haul the
sled up after them. This was the only dangerous moment. Again, the place was safe enough for the climbers
themselves. If they had slipped out of their steps, they
would certainly have gone down to the bottom of the
bowl without being able to save themselves, but it
would not have done very much harm. For Jan, trussed
up on the sled, it was a very different matter. If they
had let him go, he would have gone down much
faster, head first on his back, and certainly broken his
neck at the bottom. But they took the risk and got
away with it again. The second pair anchored the sled
about thirty feet below the cornice. The leaders set off
once more, and standing below the cornice in their
final steps, they hacked at it with their sticks till they
brought a length of it crashing down. They hauled
themselves through the gap which they had made,
and got to their feet and looked around them. They
were standing at last on the icy windswept edge of the
plateau. Ahead, the slopes were gentle and the snow
was firm.

As soon as the sled was clear of the cornice, the
men put on their skis and the climb took on a totally
different aspect. On skis they felt far more at home
than on their feet, and more able to cope with any
new crisis which might face them. The dilemma of
which way up was less painful for Jan was also solved
at last, and with his usual resilience he soon began to
recover from the rough handling they had given him.
The main remaining worry on their minds was
simply the matter of time: the climb had taken hours
longer than they had expected, and with a thousand
feet still to go they were late for the meeting with the
Mandal men already. Jan was spared from this worry, as he was from so many others. As he had been
unconscious on and off ever since they started, he had
no idea how long they had been on the way.

The fear of missing the Mandal men made them

press on without another rest. All four of them made themselves fast to the sled with short ropes tied around their waists, and they started at top speed inland across the plateau. They had no further doubts about the route. To get to the rendezvous they had to go through a shallow dip which leads up to a chain of small lakes on the watershed between Revdal and Mandal. This dip can easily be seen from across the fjord at Furuflaten, and though none of the four men had ever been up there before, the distant view of the place had been familiar to them all their lives. When they were clear of the dangerous corniced edge, they struck off diagonally to the right up the gently rising ground. The surface was ice, covered here and there by ripples of powdery windblown snow.

Within half an hour the dip in the skyline was in sight. They climbed up into it and entered a little

closed in about them, and cut off the view of the fjord and the distant mountains behind them, they began, each in his own way, to sense for the first time the threatening atmosphere of desolation which oppresses every one of the few people who have ever ventured on to the plateau in winter. The size and the barren loneliness of the plateau appals the least sensitive of travelers. From Lyngenfjord it stretches away into Sweden and Finland, far to the eastward toward the border of Soviet Russia, and then on again beyond the narrow lowlands of Petsamo, to the White Sea and the vastness of Siberia. The valley which they entered that early morning is only on the very verge of it, and yet it is unlikely that any human being will set eyes on that place from one decade's end to the next. Whoever does so, especially when the plateau is under snow, becomes bitterly aware of the hundreds of miles

of featureless wilderness beyond him, the endless hori-
zons one after another, and every one the same; the
unimaginable numbers of silent icebound valleys and
sterile, gaunt, deserted hills. Mankind has no business
there. It is a dead world, where the affairs of the human race are of no account whatever. In war or peace,
it is always the same, and always so fiercely inimical to
life that one has to think of it, when one is enclosed
within it, as an active malignant enemy. One knows
that the human body is too frail a thing to defend itself against that kind of enemy, which attacks with
hunger and frostbite and storm blindness. One knows
all too well that the plateau can kill a man easily and
quickly and impartially, whether he is English or German or Norwegian, or patriot or traitor. Into these
dreadful surroundings the little group of men crept silently, dragging the passive, half-conscious body of Jan
behind them.

It had not been very easy to decide on a place
for the meeting, because hardly any spot on the plateau
can be distinguished from any other, and because there
was no map which showed anything more than its outline. But from Furuflaten a single steep bluff can be
seen in profile on the far horizon, and for want of
anywhere better they had told the Mandal men to
meet them at the foot of it.

They came on the place almost unexpectedly, as
they breasted a little rise in the valley floor. Before
them was a level area, a hundred yards or so across,
which was probably a lake or a bog in summer. Beyond it the valley rose again to the watershed, which
was still out of sight. On the right was the bluff. It
was quite unmistakable, the only piece of black, naked
vertical rock in sight. On top of it there was a thick
snow cornice like the icing on a cake of festive richness,
which they had seen with a telescope from the other
side. But down below, at its foot, in the valley, nobody was waiting.

They stood there aghast for a moment at this failure of their hopes. Their first thought, of course, when
they saw the empty valley, was that in spite of all their

efforts they had arrived too late and the Mandal men had gone. But it only needed a minute or two of search to show that there were no ski tracks anywhere in the valley bottom. Nobody had been there at all, certainly since the last storm had abated, and probably for years.

They all jumped to the conclusion then that something had gone wrong with their instructions about the meeting place, and that the Mandal men were waiting somewhere else. They had a hurried discussion, grouped around the sled in the valley below the bluff. It seemed extremely queer that the others should have missed the landmark, which had turned out to be even more conspicuous than they expected. A forlorn hope struck them that the men might be somewhere quite close at hand, hidden perhaps in one of the shallow deceptive hollows in the valley. Someone suggested they should raise a shout. They were strangely reluctant to do so. It seemed rash to break the deathly silence of the plateau. They had been so secretive for so long that they all felt the same absurd fear: that if they shouted, they might be heard by someone who could not be trusted. Yet of course they knew it was inconceivable that anyone could be within earshot except people on the same business as themselves. After a moment's superstitious hesitation, they all shouted in unison. But the sound fell dead, muffled by the blanket of snow; and nobody answered.

After this, each of them set off in a different direction to search for the Mandal men, leaving Jan lying where he was. To hunt for a party of men on the plateau was not such a hopeless project as it might seem. It was not a matter of finding the men themselves, but of looking for their tracks. If the men had been standing still, it would have been perfectly futile, but a party on the move would leave tracks which could be seen from hundreds of yards away; and in fact a search parallel to the Mandal valley could not miss them if they were there at all.

While Jan was left lying there alone, lashed to the sled and staring at the sky, he had time to get over

whatever disappointment he may have felt at the failure
of the meeting, and to make up his mind to the worst
that could possibly happen. As he had taken no part in
the arrangements, perhaps he was not so surprised as
the others that something had gone so obviously wrong.
He felt it had been too much to hope for all along that
there would really be men waiting for him up there,
ready to take him at once to Sweden. He had never
seriously pictured himself safely across the border within the next day or two. Besides, after the agony he
had suffered while he was being pulled up the mountain, to be allowed to lie still was such an acute relief
that nothing else seemed to matter. To lie still and rest,
and perhaps to doze a little, was all he really wanted.
He even felt rather glad that there was going to be
some delay, and that he had not got to set off again
at once. And one thing was perfectly clear to him;
whatever happened, even to save his life, he simply
could not face being taken down again.

When they came back, one by one, he could see
from the face of each of them before he spoke that
there was no sign of the Mandal party. Amandus was
the last one to return. He had been right up across the
watershed, and down to the head of the tributary valley running up out of Mandal, which was the route
they expected the Mandal men to take. There were no
tracks leading out of it. To make doubly sure, he
had skirted right around the head of it and gone out on
to a sheer bastion of rock which divides the side valley
from Mandal itself. From there, leaning out over a
vertical drop of nearly three thousand feet, he had
looked down the whole length of Mandal. He had seen
the houses scattered in the bed of the valley. There was
no sign of life among them.

Jan knew that the four men had stayed with him
already far longer than was safe. They had to get
home, quickly, or their absence was perfectly certain
to be discovered, and that would be the end of them,
and of him as well. Marius and the others, for their
part, also knew what Jan had already made up his
mind to tell them; that it was out of the question to

take him down again. It would take an impossibly
long time; they had not enough strength left to do it;
and finally, they were quite certain, as he himself was,
that he would not get to the bottom alive.

Thus the decision to abandon him on the plateau did not need very much discussion. There was
nothing else whatever to be done. It was a bitter decision for them all, especially for Marius, who blamed
himself because the meeting had been a failure. He
promised Jan he would get a message through to Mandal the moment he got home, and do everything he
could to make sure that the Mandal men would come
up and find him the next night. But he made this promise with a heavy heart, because he did not really believe
that under the open sky Jan would last through to another day. He thought all the efforts he had made were
going to end in failure, and that his hopes of redeem-
ing his own inactive part in Norway's war were never to
be fulfilled.

They searched for a place to put Jan where he
would have a little shelter, and they found a boulder
where the wind had scooped out a hole in the snow.
The hole was four feet deep, and exactly the size of a
grave. They took off their skis, and lowered him
down into it, sled and all, and then untied the lash-
ings which held him down. They gave him what little
food they had, and the remains of the bottle of brandy.

After the last of them had climbed out of the hole,
they stood grouped around it, looking down at the hag-
gard, bearded, emaciated face which grinned up at
them. Jan said he would be all right, and thanked them
as best as he could. They hated what they were doing,
and illogically hated themselves for doing it. But neither
Jan nor Marius nor any of the others felt like being
histrionic about it. One by one they said good-bye, and
turned away to put on their skis again. Amandus, as it
happened, was the last of them to go, and he always
remembered the last words that were spoken, because
they were so absurd.

"There's nothing else we can give you?" he asked
Jan.

"No thanks," Jan said. "I've got everything. Except hot and cold water."

They began the descent, feeling sure they had left him to die.

12

The Plateau

The war had not had very much effect upon Mandal
before Herr Legland's urgent message was delivered.
The place had had no interest for the Germans and they
had left it alone, so that its placid and rather primitive
and impoverished life went on much the same as
usual. It is quite difficult for a stranger to see how the
Mandal people can manage to make a living and feed
and bring up families in such a forlorn and isolated
home. There are millions of people, of course, even in
Europe, who live happily enough without any road to
connect them with civilization, and a good many of
them even prefer it. But the situation of Mandal seems
to have nothing in its favor. The men go fishing, but
their jetty is far away from either the fishing grounds
or the open sea or the markets. They also farm, but
their land is snow covered and frozen for eight months
of the year and the valley faces north: on every other
side it is so steeply hemmed in by hills that the sun
only shines into it when it is high. Only a little distance
to the west, the Lyngen Alps attract tourists who
provide a rich annual harvest; but Mandal has no spec-
tacular allurements to offer to visitors, and so any stranger who comes there is a nine days' wonder.

But in spite of all this, between six and seven
hundred people do live there, and they do not want to
live anywhere else. They are far from rich, but their

houses and farms are neat and tidy, and they themselves are not by any means lacking in self-respect.
Their houses are scattered all up the valley for a distance of about ten miles from the jetty and shop at
the seaward end. There is a road which connects them,
and at least one motor truck which runs up and down
it in summer but can never go farther afield. A mile
and a half up from the jetty is the school; and it was
this school which became the headquarters of Mandal's efforts in rescuing Jan.

The schoolmaster, Herr Nordnes, was a local man
himself and he had lived there all his life. He was another disciple in learning of Herr Legland, which no
doubt was the reason why Legland chose him to or-
ganize the rescue. He knew everybody who lived in the
valley, and almost everything that went on there, and
practically all the young men in the place had received
the whole of their education from him and regarded
him still as their teacher. He himself was in middle
age, but there could not have been a better choice for a
job which called for the mobilization of the valley's
youth.

When he got Legland's message and had given
himself time to think it over, he went to call on a few
of his recent pupils and told them what he had heard
and what was needed. They responded eagerly. In spite
of the isolation of Mandal, and the fact that most
Mandal people had not seen a German soldier or a
German ship or even an aircraft, and had heard no
authentic news of the world outside for years, there was
much of the same feeling there as on the west side of
Lyngenfjord: that nobody had had a chance so far to
show what he could do to help the war. Nordnes had no
lack of volunteers. His only embarrassment, in fact, was
to prevent the news spreading too quickly, and to avoid
having too many people who wanted to take some part
in this novel adventure. Yet their enthusiasm was surprising, because the appeal for help, as it reached them,
was quite impersonal. They did not have the incentive
of having seen Jan, and had no idea what kind of person he was. The whole story was third or fourth hand.

Not even Legland had seen him, and nor had the messenger. The only reason for thinking that he deserved their help at all was that Legland had said so, and had told Nordnes that the man who was in trouble had come all the way from England.

The Mandal men would have been more than human, in these circumstances, if they had not pointed out, as their first reaction, that to take an injured man to Sweden was not so easy as it looked. The people in Tromsö and Lyngseidet, they thought, probably had no real idea of the difficulties of what they were asking Mandal to do. They might have looked at a map and seen the frontier on it, twenty-five miles away, and imagined some kind of fence with Swedish frontier guards who would take care of Jan on the spot. They probably did not realize that there was nothing there whatever, except cairns at intervals of miles, so that you could cross the border without ever knowing you had done it, and plunge down into endless forests on the Swedish side where you might be lost for weeks without seeing a house or a road. There were no defenses on the frontier simply because it was so difficult to cross that no defenses were needed.

Having registered their protest, and suggested quite rightly that Lapps were better qualified to make the actual journey, they were perfectly willing to try it themselves if it was really necessary; and they were willing in any case to meet the Furuflaten men at the rendezvous they suggested, and to look after the injured man when he was handed over. They almost certainly felt some satisfaction at being asked to pull chestnuts out of the fire on behalf of a place like Furuflaten, which had always affected to despise Mandal because it was not on the road.

During the week which elapsed after the first message from Legland, while the gale was blowing which imprisoned Jan in Revdal, the Mandal people heard nothing more about what was happening. They went on with the ordinary chores of early spring, and probably their first enthusiasm faded. The whole story only existed for them in the form of a single sudden visit by

a messenger. It began to seem likely that the organization had found some other way of moving their man, or
that he had died or been captured, and that they were
not going to be asked to do anything after all. It was
disappointing, and made them feel a little foolish.

This was the situation when the second urgent
message arrived by telephone. It was very obscure: the
parcel Herr Nordnes was expecting was being sent at
once. It told them nothing of what was happening in
Furuflaten, whether the Germans were hot on the trail,
or whether the man they were expected to look after
was seriously ill or not. They understood, of course,
that it was impossible to say more on the telephone, but
it did leave them entirely in the dark. The only shade
of meaning it conveyed was one of urgency; and urgency, in that context, suggested that the Germans
were suspicious.

However, what it asked them to do was clear
enough, and Herr Nordnes rounded up his first party of
volunteers and told them the job was on again. They
were all men in their early twenties, whom he had
chosen because they had been intelligent and resource-
ful at school, and because they were fit and strong.
There had never been any question of him climbing
up to the plateau himself, partly because he was a
generation older than the climbers he had chosen and
would only have held them back, and more especially
because he was one of the very few people in Mandal
who had to be at work exactly on time in the morning.
But his volunteers were still willing, and all said they
could make the climb that night. There was still no
news of the Lapps from the ski-runner who had set
off from Kaafjord to find them; but at least they could
take charge of Furuflaten's stranger till they heard if
the Lapps were coming. Each of them went off to
make his preparations: to change his clothes and wax
his skis and pack a rucksack, and perhaps to get a
little sleep before he started.

It was at this precise moment that a strange boat
was sighted approaching Mandal. This was a very rare
event, and plenty of people watched the boat, some

with telescopes and binoculars, from the houses near the bottom of the valley. As it approached the jetty, they saw something which was to put the whole valley in a state of turmoil and apprehension: there was a party of German soldiers on board it. The boat reached the jetty, and the Germans came ashore; and a number of people who were in the know put on their skis and pelted up to the schoolhouse to warn Herr Nordnes. As the news spread up the valley, all the people he had consulted began to converge on the school to talk about this sinister development.

They all took it for granted that it had something to do with the plot which was afoot. It seemed certain that the organization in Furuflaten had been broken up, and that the Germans knew that Mandal was involved in it; or else that somebody higher in the organization, in Tromsö perhaps, had been arrested and that the Germans were planning a simultaneous raid on both sides of the mountain. At all events, it would have been crazy to make the climb that night, before the Germans had shown some sign of what they meant to do. Herr Nordnes himself knew that his own name was the only one in Mandal so far which anyone outside could connect with the affair, and he did the only thing he could do: he told all the others to stay at home and say nothing; and for himself, he resolved that if he was arrested he would try not to give them away whatever was done to him.

That evening, the people of Mandal watched every move which the Germans made; but they seemed to be in no hurry to do anything at all. The second wave of news which spread up the valley reported that there were only six soldiers and an n.c.o. This seemed to suggest that they had come to arrest one single individual. But later rumor said that they were taking over a house as a billet, down by the jetty. Nobody knew whether it was for one night or for good, but obviously if there was going to be an arrest, it was not going to happen before nightfall. That night while Marius and his party were hauling the sled up Revdal and searching the plateau, nobody was sleeping soundly in Mandal, except perhaps the Germans. When Amandus looked down from the top of the buttress in the early morning, the silent houses he saw far down below him were kept silent by anxiety and fear.

But during the night nothing happened at all. The Germans stayed in their billet, and in the morning they sallied forth and began a house-to-house check of all the inhabitants of Mandal. On the whole this relieved the tension. It pointed to a general vague suspicion of Mandal as a whole, rather than something definite against a particular person. But it meant that nobody could go away from home until the check of his own house had been completed, and to judge by the desultory way that the Germans went to work, this would put a stop to any journey to the frontier for several days. It also made it impossible for the present for anyone to go over to Lyngseidet by boat to find out what had happened; and even to ring up Herr Legland would be asking for trouble, in case he had been arrested.

The whole thing remained a mystery all that day. Whatever way Nordnes and the other conspirators looked at it, it was hard to believe that after years without a garrison, the sudden arrival of even a section of Germans on the very evening when the ascent of the plateau was planned could be simply a coincidence. Yet nothing the Germans did, once they had landed, seemed to have any bearing on the plot, or to suggest in any way that they knew what was going on.

This particular mystery, as it happened, was never solved. To this day it still seems incredible that the Germans arrived there by chance; yet there is no reason to think they had any suspicion, at that particular moment, that Jan had been taken across to the east side of Lyngenfjord. The last time they had seen him was when he was skiing through Lyngseidet, and that was nearly three weeks earlier. But perhaps the fact that he had slipped through their grasp and disappeared had brought it home to somebody in the local command that the routes to the frontier were not very

well controlled. Perhaps somebody else had had a rap
on the knuckles. The somewhat pathetic little garrison
sent to Mandal, as well as the motorboats which suddenly appeared on Lyngenfjord, may have been part of
a general tightening of the grip on the frontier, an indirect result of Jan's journey rather than a deliberate
search for him. If anyone knows the answer to this, it
can only be some German officer.

However, the immediate mystery for Herr Nordnes was cleared up to some extent by an urgent message which arrived that night. It had come by a devious
route, but it had originated from Marius, and it told
Nordnes that Jan had been left at the meeting place on
the plateau and begged him to have him collected without delay. It also told him, by the mere fact that it had
been sent, that there was nothing wrong in the rest of
the organization and that they did not even know that
the Germans had come to Mandal. He went out to
round up his team again, and to see whether they
thought it was safe to start at once. But before the
point was decided, it began to snow.

Standing outside the schoolhouse in Mandal, one
can see almost the whole of the route to the plateau
which they intended to use. As Marius and Amandus
had expected, it lies up the side valley which leads out
of Mandal on its southern side. This lesser valley is
called Kjerringdal, the word *kjerring* meaning an old
woman or hag, to correspond with the man of Mandal.
Kjerringdal rises steeply, in a series of gleaming curved
terraces of snow, and in spring almost the whole of it
is swept by avalanches; but there is one route up it
clear of the avalanche tracks which is known to the
local men. It ends in a wide couloir. From Mandal the
rim of the couloir stands against the sky, three thousand feet above; and two miles beyond the rim is the
place where Jan was lying.

That night, the snow clouds gathered first above
the head of Mandal, and then, even as Nordnes and
his men were watching them and debating the weather, they swept up from the south across the plateau,
and poured over the edge of the couloir and down into

Kjerringdal. Minute by minute they grew thicker and
nearer, blotting out the high terraces one by one, till
the clouds from Kjerringdal joined with the ones from
Mandal and swirled around the vertical crag which
divides the two valleys. A few moments later they were
overhead, and the snow began to fall, softly and thickly, on the floor of the valley where the men were standing. Soon there was nothing but snowflakes to be seen.

None of them liked to think of a man lying ill and
unprotected and helpless up there in the heart of the
clouds; but falling snow put an end to whatever hopes
they had of reaching him for the present. The German
garrison might have been avoided, and even in snow
the ascent of Kjerringdal might not have been impossible; but to find the meeting place would have been out
of the question. Nobody in Mandal knew exactly where
it was. They would have to depend on seeing the steep
bluff which the Furuflaten message had described, and
to begin to search for it when they could not see more
than a few yards in front of them would be futile and
suicidal. There was nothing for it but to wait till the
snowstorm ended.

It went on snowing all night, and all the morning.
Going about their business in the valley the following
day none of them had much hope for the man on the
top of the mountain. Perhaps they regretted then they
had not gone up on the night that the Germans came.
As it turned out, they could have done it without being
caught; but nobody could have known that at the time.
Now, everything depended on the snow. They were
ready to go the moment it showed the first sign of easing. It was simply a question of whether the man would
survive till then.

The chance came on the third night after Marius
had left Jan up there. There were breaks in the clouds
that evening, and the local men, with their knowledge
of Mandal weather, believed it would be clear before
the morning. The party of four volunteers assembled.
The Germans had been watched and counted to make
sure they were all out of sight in the billet at the foot of
the valley. Everything seemed auspicious.

The ascent of Kjerringdal went off without any serious trouble, though under the best of conditions it is not a safe or easy climb at that time of year. From time to time Nordnes caught sight of the men toiling on up the valley, picking their course to avoid the avalanche tracks. After four hours, on skis all the way, they got to the rim of the plateau. The snow had stopped by then, as they had hoped, and they struck off right-handed to make the level trek across the watershed and then down toward Revdal.

They saw the steep bluff well ahead of them. A series of gentle gullies and frozen lakes led down to the foot of it, and they ran down into the shallow valley which Marius and his party had reached three nights before. The fresh snow which had fallen lay thick over everything. The valley seemed just as deserted and still as the rest of the plateau. There were no tracks and no sign whatever that anyone had ever been there. They searched the foot of the bluff, and the whole of the valley bed above it and below, but they could not find anything at all. They scoured the plateau around about, shouting, but there was no answer. For two hours they hunted far and wide; but then they had to give it up and make back for the head of Kjerringdal again, in order to be at home before the Germans began their day's work of checking the houses. The ski-run down Kjerringdal was very fast, and they were back in Mandal by the time the place was stirring.

When they all talked over this night's expedition with Nordnes, the only conclusion they could come to was that the man who had been left up there had gone off somewhere by himself. They still knew very little about him. They had heard he was crippled, but for all they could tell, he might still have been able to drag himself along. It seemed most likely that when the snow had started, he had tried to get down again on the Revdal side to look for shelter. It had also crossed their minds, of course, that he might have died and been buried by the snow. In fact, they thought anyone who had stayed on the plateau for the past three days would almost certainly be dead; but they dismissed the idea that he had died anywhere near the rendezvous, because they thought they would have found his body. There had not been any avalanche up there, and there was very little drifting, and they would have expected a dead man's body to show as a visible mound on the snowfield. Even if he had dug himself in and then been buried, there should have been something to show where he had done it. But there was nothing at all. He had simply disappeared.

For all practical purposes, Mandal just then was entirely cut off from the outside world. The Germans had been making strict inquiries about anyone they found was not at home, and they expected an explanation of where every man was and what he was doing. Until they had finished their slow and laborious progress from house to house up the whole of the valley, it was obvious that they would not let anyone leave it; and Nordnes could not send a messenger over the fjord to tell Herr Legland what had happened. He could not use the telephone, either. It had always been tapped on and off, and it was sure to be tapped, or simply cut off, while the German search was going on; and the whole mystery was too complicated to discuss in disguised language without any prearranged code. If Nordnes had been able to have five minutes' conversation with Marius, everything would have been easy, but they might as well have been on different continents; and besides, at that time neither of them knew who was the organizer of the other village's part in the affair. The only way of communication between them was through Legland, and for the present that way was blocked.

Without any help or advice from outside, the only thing the Mandal men could do was to try again. A second party therefore made the long climb on the following night, the fourth since Jan had been abandoned on the plateau. They regarded it as almost a hopeless effort; but Mandal, in the person of Herr Nordnes, had promised it would do its best, and besides, while there was any chance at all that there was a man alive up there, none of them could have slept easily in their beds.

This time, when they got to the valley below the bluff, it was still covered with the ski tracks from the night before. They extended the search farther down toward the edge of the drop into Revdal, and inland across the plateau. Every few yards they broke the oppressive silence of the plateau with a shout, and listened while it died again to silence.

Somebody had decided on a password which had been given both to Jan and the Mandal men. Presumably as a tribute to Jan's English training, the Mandal men were to identify themselves to him by saying "Hallo, gentleman." People in Norway often suppose that the word gentleman can be used as a form of address in the singular, as indeed it could if there were any logic in the English language. That night the plateau rang with this repeated cry but nobody in either Mandal or Furuflaten spoke any English at all, and so there was nobody there who would have thought it odd or ludicrous; except Jan, and he could not hear it. Toward morning, the party retreated again by way of Kjerringdal without finding anything. As they went down, the weather was worsening.

This second sortie had made it clear that it was no use to search any more without some kind of consultation with Furuflaten. To put a final end to any thought of another expedition, the snow began again, and during the day the wind got up and increased to a blizzard. This was far worse than the calm snowfall of two days before. In the sheltered valley, the temperature fell abruptly and visibility was restricted, and any outside work became impossible. On the plateau, as the Mandal people knew from generations of experience, no search party would have a hope of finding anything; it would be all they could do to move at all against the wind, or in fact, after a very short time, even to keep themselves alive.

But the blizzard did have one helpful consequence, in that it hampered the German troops as much as anyone. They could not keep their eye any

longer on the whole of the foot of the valley, even if
they did venture out into the blinding snow; and under
the unexpected cover of this storm, a skier slipped
out of the valley and brought the news of Mandal's
plight to friends in Kaafjord. From there, after a day's
delay in which a boat was found which could cross
the fjord in such wild weather, the news reached Herr
Legland, and he sent a message at once to Marius.

This message undoubtedly was a terrible shock to
Marius. It reached him in Furuflaten when the blizzard
was still at its height and had already been blowing for
days. It meant only one thing to him: that after all
Jan had suffered, and all that had been risked for him,
he was dead. It was exactly a week since Marius had
said good-bye to him when he put him in the snow
grave on the plateau. All that time, as he had not heard
anymore, he had taken it for granted that the Mandal
men had found him, and he had even thought of him
safe already in a Swedish hospital. It was dreadful for
Marius to think that nobody had ever come to take
him out of that hole again. His own knowledge of the
arctic mountains, and the wisdom he had learned
from older people, all made him certain that nobody
had ever survived, or ever could survive, a week of
snow and storm on the plateau, under the open sky. He
could have wept to think of the pitifully inadequate
protection Jan had had: two blankets, and a canvas bag
which was not even waterproof, and not more than a
day's supply of food. He hated to think what Jan
must have thought of him when he knew his end was
coming.

Marius's imagination would not let him rest on the
day when he got the message. He took the news around
to all the people he could tell, those who had helped in
different ways. They were all of the same opinion: that
it was a pity it had to end that way, but after all, everyone had done his best. Nobody even suggested that
Jan might still be alive. Yet Marius knew all the time,
in the back of his mind, that he would have to go up to
the plateau again that night, whatever the weather, and
whatever the risk of being seen and arrested by the

Germans when it was really too late to matter. Of course he had not forgotten the solemn promise he had made to Jan; and assuming that Jan was dead, the promise had been broken. He had to go, if only to see for himself. He disliked the idea of leaving Jan's body up there where it lay, till the spring thaw exposed the last remains of it. He wondered if Jan would have left him a message, written on paper perhaps, which the thaw would destroy. Perhaps he has some idea, as people do when the death of a friend leaves them remorseful, of making his peace with Jan by going to look at his body. At any rate, whether it was rational or not, and whether it was suicidally dangerous or not, he knew he was going.

It was a question who would come with him. To go alone would have added a lot to the danger: two people on a mountain in a blizzard are always more than twice as safe as one. But of the three men who had been with him before, Alvin Larsen and Olaf Lanes were away again fishing, and probably storm-stayed somewhere down the coast, and Amandus Lillevoll was having such pain with his broken ribs that it was foolish to think of him making the climb again. There were no other men in the village in the know, only women: his own sisters and mother, and families of the men who had come with him.

Olaf Lanes had several sisters, and one of them was called Agnethe. Agnethe knew Marius well, and she was fond of him, and so was he of her. When she heard that he was determined to go that night, she knew quite well that if nobody else would go with him, he would go alone; and rather than let him do that, she went and told him firmly that she was coming too. Probably if any other girl had said the same thing, he would have refused her offer without a second thought. It was certainly not an expedition for a girl. But Agnethe was as good as any man on skis, and she was strong as well as pretty; and, perhaps even more important, she was the only person that day who really understood the whole depth of what he was feeling, and agreed with him that it was right to go. He pos-

sibly needed sympathy just then even more than physical help. She offered him both, and he was grateful;
and because there was really no sensible alternative,
he agreed to let her come.

At dusk, which was all that was left by then of the
vanishing nights, these two embarked on what was to
be the last crossing of Lyngenfjord to Revdal. Amandus had come with them to help them to handle the
boat and to look after it at Revdal. The crossing was
wet and wild, and the small boat under sail was beaten
down by heavy squalls from the mountains. But at
least it was hidden from German eyes as long as the
snow went on falling. They reached the other shore
drenched and cold but safe, and beached the boat
about half a mile south of Revdal. Agnethe and Marius landed.

They took a new route up the mountain. It looked
easier for unladen climbers than the one which Marius
had taken with the sled, but it included some pitches
of simple rock climbing, in narrow chimneys, on which
the sled would have been a hopeless hindrance. Marius
looked after Agnethe with affection and admiration, but
she needed no help from him. On rock she was more
agile than he was, and perhaps she was even more
anxious to reach the plateau and see the worst, so that
his mind would be set at rest.

They climbed the first steep two thousand feet
very quickly. But on the steep face they were more or
less in shelter. When they had almost got up to the rim
of the plateau, they began to hear a new note in the
wind above them, and when they looked up through
the murk they could see the snow blowing over the
edge. It looked like hard gray pellets, and it shot over
in jets with a power and speed which warned them
that the dangerous part of the climb was only beginning.

When they crossed the rim and stood up on the
level surface beyond it, the wind snatched at their
clothes and threw them off their balance and drowned
their voices. The air was so full of whirling particles
of snow that it took their breath away and they felt as

if they were suffocating. Both of them, of course, were
properly dressed, in windproof trousers and *anuraks*
with hoods; but the snow lashed the exposed parts of
their faces with such violent pain that they could not
bear to turn unprotected into the wind. Marius shouted
to Agnethe, half-persuaded himself that what they
were doing was madness; but she was already untying
her skis, which had been bound together for carrying.
She dropped them on the shifting surface, and bent
down to buckle on the bindings.

The way for the last three miles from there to the
rendezvous was against the wind. If it had not been
so, it certainly would have been more than foolish to go
on, because of the danger of overreaching themselves
and being unable to return. They pulled their hoods
down as far as they would go, and covered their
mouths with their hands to ward off the snow and
make breathing possible. Marius set off in the lead,
because he knew the way, and marched on with his
head bent low, snatching a painful glance ahead of
him now and then. Agnethe followed close after him in
his tracks. Neither of them could see normally or hear
anything but the howling of the wind, and their sense
of touch was numbed by cold. When the senses are
numbed, a mental numbness cannot be avoided. In
this state they went on and on, yard by yard into the
wilderness, thinking no farther ahead than the next
step and the one after that. They climbed with that
thoughtless stubbornness, against all reason, which is
often the mainspring of great deeds: Marius driven
on by his own compelling conscience, and Agnethe by
her sympathy and love.

When they came to the bluff they could see the loom
of it above them through the snow mist; but even
Marius had to hesitate before he could find the boulder
where Jan had been laid. Everything was changed. The
fresh snowfall and the high wind had made new drifts,
exposed new rocks and hidden others. The boulder
which had stood conspicuously clear of the surface
was almost buried, and in the lee of it, where the open
hole had been, there was not a smooth windswept

surface. The puzzle of why the Mandal men had found nothing there was solved: there was nothing whatever to be seen. Yet Marius felt certain of his bearings. He was sure he had found the right boulder, and that Jan could not have moved, and that therefore, his body was buried far down below that virgin surface. He took off his skis and went down on his knees in the soft snow and began to dig. He scratched the snow away with his hands. Agnethe crouched beside him in an agony of cold. She was exhausted.

When Marius had dug away three feet of snow, the rest collapsed into a cavity underneath, and he knew he was right. He cleared it away, and saw Jan's ghastly waxen face blow him. The eyes were shut, and the head was covered with rime.

"Don't look," he said to Agnethe. "He's dead."

At the sound of his voice, Jan stirred.

"I'm not dead, damn you," he said, in a feeble voice but with every sign of indignation.

Then he opened his eyes, and saw the astounded face of Marius peering down at him, and he grinned.

"You can't kill an old fox," he said.

13

Buried Alive

Nobody can give an exact account of what happened
to Jan during all the weeks he spent lying alone on the
plateau. By the time he had leisure to look back on it,
his memory was confused. He had the same difficulty
that one has in trying to bring back to mind the events
and one's feelings during a serious illness; and in fact,
of course, he was seriously ill all the time. Some incidents and impressions were perfectly clear to him, but
as he remembered them they had no context; they were
isolated, like distant memories of childhood, and he
had only a hazy idea of what had led up to them, or
what followed after. But most of the episodes he remembered were confirmed in one way or another by
the people who visited him up there from time to time.
In general, oddly enough, he had no impression of
being bored. Once when somebody asked him how
he had passed the time, he said he had never been so
busy in his life. And one thing, at least, which is perfectly certain is the length of time this extraordinary
ordeal lasted. He lay in the sleeping bag in the snow for
no less than 27 consecutive days, from the night of the
25th of April, when Marius took him up to the plateau,
till the night of the 22nd of May, when they were to
carry him down again in despair.

That first week, in the snow grave, was the worst
in some respects, partly because he was not so used to

that way of living as he became toward the end, and partly because he was forced to believe, for the second time, that his friends had abandoned him, or lost him, or all been killed themselves. He did not think he would ever get out of the grave again.

At first, he had been so relieved to be allowed to lie still that he said good-bye to Marius and the other three men without any fear of another spell of solitude. He settled down in the sleeping bag on the sled, with the wall of snow on one side of him and the rock on the other, and the small segment of sky up above, and he thought he would go to sleep. But only too soon this mood of contentment was driven away by the cold. It was much too cold to sleep. During the climb the sleeping bag and the blankets had got wet, and in the hole in the snow the moisture froze them stiff. They were to remain either wet or frozen for the whole of the time he was there, and he discovered one thing at once which was to plague him through all those weeks: he could never sleep, because the cold always woke him and he had to keep moving inside the blankets to ward off another attack of frostbite. At the best, he could only fall into an uneasy doze.

Apart from the cold, the sled made a very uncomfortable bed. It had been a mistake to make the top out of narrow slats with spaces in between them. There were only two layers of blanket and one of canvas, besides his clothes, between him and the wooden slats; and because he had to keep moving he soon got sores all over his back and sides which made the discomfort infinitely worse.

During the first two days and night, before it began to snow, he kept imagining that among the occasional whispering sounds of the plateau he heard the hiss of skis. Sometimes he shouted to the people he thought were there. But this was not the kind of hallucination he had had after the avalanche. On the plateau, his brain was quite clear. Perhaps the sounds were made by little snowballs rolling down the snow-covered scree at the foot of the bluff above him.

As soon as it started to snow, on the second night

he lay in the hole, he knew that his chance of being found was very small, at least till the snow stopped falling; and there was an extra worry added to this, because at about the same time he finished the few bits of food they had left him, and he was beginning to get very hungry.

By that time his movements and the heat of his body had made a cavity in the snow, and the sled had sunk deeper than it had been. The fresh snowfall soon covered his body. He could brush it off his face and his head, but in the narrow hole he could not throw it off the rest of him. Slowly it sifted over his trunk and legs till they were encased in a kind of tunnel, bridged over by a thickening layer of snow which he could not move. For some hours he kept a hole clear to the surface above his head, so that he could still see the open air above him. But the snow grew deeper and deeper till he could not reach up to the surface any more even with his arm stretched out above him. Then the snow closed over the opening, and buried him alive.

He was buried for either four or five days. What kept him alive is a mystery. It was not hope, because he had none, and it was not any of the physical conditions which are usually supposed to be essential to human life. Perhaps it is nearest to the truth to put his survival down to a stubborn distaste for dying in such gruesome circumstances.

He lay on his back in a little vault in the snow. At the sides and above his body there were a few inches of space, and above his head there was over a foot, but there was not enough room for him to draw up his knees or reach down to touch his feet. A dim light filtered down from above, like the light below the surface of the sea. He had no trouble in breathing, because the snow above him was fresh and porous, but he lay all the time in fear that the roof would fall in and pin his arms down and cover his mouth and choke him.

He could imagine quite well the change that had taken place on the surface of the plateau in such a heavy snowfall, and he knew that even if the Mandal men did come to look for him, it was very unlikely that they would find him before the summer thaw exposed his body. Of course, he knew he could not live till then, because in the first stages of the thaw the snow would become compacted and impervious and he would be very, very slowly suffocated.

The only vestige of physical comfort he had in all this time was the dregs of the bottle of brandy. There was not very much in it when he was left there, but as he was weak and starving, less than a mouthful of it was enough to make him slightly drunk. He made it last out for some time after the food was gone. When everything became intolerable, he had the bottle to think about. He would put off taking a sip for hours, so that he could enjoy the anticipation of the warmth going down his throat; and when at last he grasped the precious bottle, and wrestled weakly with the cork, and struggled in the confines of the grave to tilt it to his mouth, the spoonful of raw spirit dulled his pains and made the next hour or two slip past more easily. At times he was even struck by the humor of lying buried in one's grave and swigging a bottle of brandy. But of course the moment came when there was only one more spoonful in the bottle. This he kept as if it were his only link with life, and it was still there when Marius relieved him.

There was one benefit of being buried. Certainly it prevented the Mandal men from finding him, and thereby was nearly the end of him; but to compensate for this, it protected him from everything that happened on the surface. If he had been exposed, the blizzard after the snowfall would have killed him; but in his grave he was no more aware of the howling wind than he was of the shouts of the Mandal party. The blizzard blew over him, but down in the vault in the snow it was always perfectly silent and perfectly calm, and the temperature was always steady, a few degrees below zero.

So he lay while the days and nights passed over. He had no inclination by then to indulge himself with daydreams, or to philosophize as he had in the hut at

Revdal. His mind was occupied with the minute details of physical existence: to keep moving, to be on the watch for frostbite, to try to ease the pain of his feet and the sores on his back; to try the impossible task of keeping his body in some state of sanitation; to stop the snow roof falling down, to prevent the bottle of brandy falling over. Each of these tasks became an absorbing activity which occupied him for hours on end, and each one of them was an important part of his conscious effort not to die. He added to them, typically, the task of cleaning the revolver which he still wore in its holster. When any of the tasks were accomplished for the moment, he felt he had warded off death for a few more minutes. He sometimes visualized death as a physical being who prowled about him. He parried the lunges this creature made at him, and he was proud of himself when he thrust off another of its attacks. It did not occur to him then that he might have welcomed death's more compassionate advances.

When Marius broke through the snow above him he was dozing, and he heard his voice in a dream, as he often had before. In the dream he was annoyed that the voice said he was dead. It seemed too bad of Marius to suggest that he had lost the battle with death, when he had been trying so hard to win it, so he denied it hotly. Then he opened his eyes and it was real: and Marius looked so surprised that he laughed and, half-conscious, he said out loud the Norwegian proverb which had been running in his head. "You can't kill an old fox, you know. You can't kill an old fox."

This voice from the dead did in fact almost paralyze Marius for a moment while he reorganized his thoughts. A surge of relief made his heart beat faster; but immediately after it came the fore-knowledge of the problems which had come to life again with Jan. Jan himself was beyond being surprised by then by anything that happened: it did not strike him as particularly strange, though it was pleasant, to see a hooded and yet unmistakably feminine and attractive face looking down at him by the side of Marius. Marius and Agnethe scraped away more snow till Marius could climb down into the hole and clear a space around Jan so that he had a little more freedom to move about. He had brought food with him, more as an offering to fate than with any hope of using it. He fed Jan with bread and bits of fish, while he was explaining how the Mandal men had tried to find him. He had also brought more brandy and some tobacco. Jan could not eat much, but he had a craving for a cigarette, and Marius rolled him one and crouched over him to shelter him while he lit it.

Puffing at this cigarette, while the snow drifted into the hole and the wind shrieked overhead in the gray half-darkness, Jan began to feel almost himself again. It was the belief that he was forgotten that always brought him down to his lowest depths. Now his own hardships faded, and he noticed that Agnethe was in terrible distress. By then, in fact, she was so cold that she could hardly speak. As soon as Jan realized what she was suffering, and all on his behalf, he insisted that they should leave him and get down to the fjord again while they were still able to do it.

Marius himself knew he could not do any good by staying. The only useful thing he could do was to go down and make perfectly certain, as quickly as possible, of getting a large enough party up from one side of the mountain or the other to move Jan away from where he was. The message from Mandal had said they would make the climb again as soon as the weather allowed it. Marius told Jan of this, and to help them to find him if they did come he made a flag by tying a piece of cloth to a ski-stick which he stuck in the snow by the side of the hole. So, after staying with Jan for only half an hour, they left him again with this forlorn signal flapping wildly in the storm above him.

As ever, Marius's unrelenting conscience asked him whether he had done all that was humanly possible, and this time he had to admit to himself that he had not. There was still the slight chance that the Man-

dal men might be on their way up at that very minute.
It was true that the weather had not improved at all,
but he felt that he ought to be there, just in case they
had chosen to come that night, to make sure that
they found the flag. He could not afford to waste time
by waiting. The only way to make sure of it quickly
was to go on toward Mandal and see if they were coming. Accordingly, instead of turning back down the
wind and downhill toward Revdal and home, he and
Agnethe faced up into the wind again and climbed
on toward the watershed.

In those awful conditions, this was a very brave
thing to do, and like many brave and admirable deeds
it was also foolhardy. Agnethe agreed with it willingly
when Marius proposed it, but she very nearly died as a
result. They reached the watershed, fighting against the
wind for every step. Up there, they lost their way, but
were saved by a sudden momentary clearance. They
pressed on and got right across to the rim of the couloir
at the head of Kjerringdal. Here there is a small isolated
rock from which one can see in clear weather right
down to the bottom of Mandal. Marius clung to the lee
of this rock and peered down into the depths below.
This was the point at which the Mandal men would
come up out of Kjerringdal on to the plateau. But that
night, although it was light by then, he could only see a
few yards down the valley through the scudding snow.
There was nobody in sight. While he was searching
over the edge, Agnethe collapsed by the side of the
rock behind him. When he saw her and turned back to
her in alarm, he found she was unconscious.

Both their lives depended then on whether he
could revive her, because of course he would never have
left her. He set about it in the most drastic way. He
shook her limp body, and hit her and slapped her face.
He believed, he said afterward, that apart from anything else this would make her angry, and that anger
would improve her circulation. Whether this was the
way it worked or not, it did bring her back to consciousness, and as soon as she gave any sign of life

he dragged her to her feet and started off, half-carrying
her, determined whatever happened to keep her on the
move.

Luckily, going down wind was infinitely easier
than going against it, and once they had got back the
first mile across the watershed the rest of the way was
downhill. Luckily also, although the climb and the cold
had used up the last of Agnethe's physical strength, she
had an unlimited strength of will. Many people who
are exhausted by exposure lose even the will to help
those who try to rescue them. If Agnethe had resisted

the rough treatment Marius gave her as he hauled her and bullied her along, or if she had ever succumbed to the insidious temptation to give up, neither of them would ever have been seen alive again. But there was a tough arctic quality in the girl which kept her going, and between them they won through to the head of Revdal and staggered down to the shore where Amandus was keeping the boat.

The climb did her no permanent physical harm, but the memory of the sight of Jan lying in the hole was to haunt her for years. It had been such a terrible sight that she thought when she saw him that he had nothing left to live for and would have been better dead.

14

Attempt on the Frontier

When a message reached Mandal to say that Jan was still up on the plateau and still alive, they began to make final preparations for an all-out attempt on the frontier as soon as the blizzard died down. For the last few days, they had not been expecting to have to try it, because when they looked up toward the loom of the mountains through the wildly driving snow, it was incredible that up there, away beyond the very top of Kjerringdal, there could be a man still living. But the fact that he had survived so far made it seem all the more worthwhile to try to save him. The preparations were rather grim. They knew they were running a big risk of never coming back, either because of some disaster on the plateau or through getting lost or interned in Sweden. But if a sick man could exist on the plateau, it would have been a disgrace to admit that four fit men could not try to move him across it to safety.

The plan for getting the Lapps to help had fallen through, at least for the time being. The ski-runner who had gone out from Kaafjord to look for them had come back, just missing the worst of the blizzard, but the news he had brought was discouraging. The reindeer were still much farther away than they usually were at that time of year. He had followed their migration track back across the plateau to the southeast for over fifty miles before he sighted the vast herds, halted and digging for the moss beneath the snow. The Lapps he was looking for were camped among them in their deerskin tents.

He was criticized afterward for not having made allowance for the queer psychology of Lapps. He had broached the subject of Jan and the journey to the frontier while he was sitting with the Lapps in a tent which was full of women and children; and the Lapps had simply refused to say yes or no. They were friendly, as Lapps always are, but they would not give the least sign of whether they might be willing, or even whether they really understood what they were being asked to do. People who knew the Lapps well, being wise after the event, said they would never commit themselves to any decision while their families were listening.

Certainly the mental processes of Lapps are very strange. They do not seem to grasp the idea of expressing an opinion. On a matter of fact which is within their own experience they will be quite dogmatic and clearheaded; but their minds do not work in terms of probabilities, and if they are asked whether something is likely to happen, they are genuinely puzzled and think the question is foolish. People tell the story of a Norwegian tourist who wanted to fish for salmon and asked a Lapp if he thought he would be able to get one in a particular local river; and the Lapp, who knew him well, shook his head with a sigh, and answered, "Really, I sometimes think you Norwegians are crazy. How could I answer a question like that? Of course there are plenty of salmon in the river, but why should you think I can tell if you can catch them?"

This curious limitation naturally makes it difficult for a Lapp to make up his mind what he is going to do. When there is a question of immediate action, provided it is something to do with reindeer or the technique of wresting a living from the arctic, he may be a shrewder man than anyone; and he can think ahead in terms of the unalterable cycles of nature, the rising and setting of the sun, the seasons and the movements of the deer. But in other matters, he is no good at all at planning things far ahead.

So the question which was put to the Kaafjord Lapps was one which they were probably incapable of answering. The ski-runner did not ask them to come at once, because he knew they could not leave their reindeer, and the herds could not be hurried. The question was whether they would help Jan when they arrived with the herds at Kaafjord, and this was too far ahead for them to contemplate. It probably bogged their minds in impossible speculations. Endless imponderable ideas would have upset them and confused them: their reindeer might be sick, the weather might be bad, they might be sick themselves: anything might happen. Nobody, in fact, could have promised more at that moment than that he would do his best when the time came, and a Lapp either cannot think in such vague terms or cannot express them in language. His answer must be precise and literal. A Lapp could only say, quite definitely, "When I get to Kaafjord, I will take a man to Sweden"; and to say a thing like that would be absurd. After all, a Lapp would reason, by that time the man might be dead; and then, if he had said he was going to take him to Sweden, he would look ridiculous.

So for the present this scheme was at a standstill. The people in Kaafjord still hoped that when the first Lapps actually arrived there, they would be able to persuade them to do the job. But the migration was late already, and the blizzard would hold it up still further. None of the herds would get there for three or four days, at least, after the weather improved. The Mandal people thought this was too long to wait, especially on the mere chance that any Lapps would agree.

The blizzard, in fact, began to moderate on the day after Marius and Agnethe made their expedition, and on the following night a third party of volunteers made the ascent of Kjerringdal. They took with them everything they could muster for a long journey, but nobody in Mandal possessed the proper equipment for a winter encampment on the plateau. The Lapps, prim-

itive though they are, would have been far more suit-
ably fitted out, with tents of hide, and clothes of reindeer skin with the hair left on, and with centuries of
experience of going to ground when the arctic weather
was at its worst. In fact, the most elaborate civilized
camping outfit would be less suited to those arctic
uplands than the Lapps' equipment, which is entirely
homemade of various parts of reindeer; and the best
which could be found in Mandal was far from elaborate. Nobody even had a tent, or a stove which would
burn in a wind, because nobody in living memory had
ever needed to make such a winter journey. But in a
place like Mandal, people never waste time in wishing
for things which they have not got; they make do with
what comes to hand. They could only hope the weather
would not be bad.

As soon as they got within sight of the meeting
place that night, they saw the flag. They hurried down
toward it on their skis, shouting the password, "Hallo,
gentleman!" For the first time, Jan heard this joyful
and comic greeting, and he shouted, "Hallo, there!" in
reply; and in a minute his solitary grave was surrounded
by helpful strangers who hacked away its walls and
dragged him bodily out on the sled to the world which
he had not seen for a week and had not expected ever
to see again.

Those of the men who had been there on either
of the earlier climbs were amazed that they had not
not found him. They thought they had actually skied
over the top of him while he was buried there; and this
is not impossible, even though he never heard them,
because four feet of snow absorbs a lot of sound, and
his senses were probably not so acute as he may have
thought they were.

Without wasting more time than it took to explain to him what they were doing, they lashed him to
the sled again and started off on their desperate bid to
cross the plateau on the way to the Swedish border.
When they climbed out of the valley, their hopes were
high, because they had found him without the delay
of searching. Even Jan, who had learned not to hope

for much, was cautiously happy to be on the move
again, and could not help thinking how few were the
miles between himself and Sweden.

But from the beginning, their progress was very
slow. The plateau is much more difficult ground for
man-hauling a sled than the flat ice fields of the Arctic
and Antarctic. None of the plateau is flat. It is covered
all over with miniature hills and valleys. Hardly any
of the hills are more than one or two hundred feet
above the valleys, but one is always going either uphill
or down. This is no obstacle to a skier, because the time
which he loses in climbing is made up on the free runs
down. But the sled could never be allowed to run.
Hauling it up the hills was slow, and going down again
it always had to be checked so that it did not get out of
control. Both were equally tiring. Once, the sled did get
away on a downward slope, and Jan careered madly
down the hill, feet first, and helpless. But luckily the
slope was smooth and the sled did not overturn, but
came to rest on a level snowfield at the bottom, with
the breathless skiers chasing close behind it.

The maze of little hills, jumbled together without
any form or pattern, also destroys any sense of direction. It is impossible to keep a straight compass course.
Probably the best way to steer is by the sun, but when
the sky is heavily overcast, as it was on that day, one has
to stop every few minutes to take bearings. In normally open country, one can take a bearing of a landmark two or three miles away, and then make toward it.
But on the plateau, one can seldom see far ahead and
there are seldom any recognizable landmarks. If one
happens from one hilltop to sight a conspicuous rock on
a distant skyline, one loses it again in the valleys, and
before one has reached it it seems to have disappeared.
There is only one way to avoid making useless devia-
tions, and that is to stop at the top of each tiny hill or
ridge and take a bearing of some stone or fold in the
snow on the next, which may be only a hundred yards
away. It takes time, and a lot of patience.

As the four men, with Jan's helpless body dragging through the snow, crept farther and farther into

this wilderness, steering south toward Sweden, the endless hills which were still ahead of them, with their
endless petty checks and obstacles, began to seem like
an impenetrable web. In forcing a way through them,
they were not limited by the mountaineer's usual worry
of being benighted. There was still a fortnight before the
sun would actually be above the horizon night and day,
but it was quite light enough for the party to keep
moving through the night. The only limit to the journey
was their own endurance. A time would come when
they would have to try to sleep, and they were so
poorly equipped that they could not expect to sleep
soundly enough to restore their strength to normal.
After a sleep, the second stage would be slower and
shorter than the first; and the first was being so des-
perately slow that a new danger began to loom
ahead: the danger of reaching the point of exhaustion
before they came to Sweden, and after they had gone
too far to be able to get home again.

So as they went on, their hopeful spirit faded, and
gave way to a growing fear that they were trying something entirely beyond their powers. None of them
wanted to be the first to admit defeat, and they went
on a long way after it was hopeless. What finally turned
the doubt into despair was the weather. During the
morning the wind had sprung up again, and the
snowclouds began to pile up and darken the southern
sky. It looked as if the improvement in the night had
only been a lull, and as if the blizzard was going to
start again, as furiously as ever. They halted on top of a
hill. They had been hauling the sled for six hours then,
apart from the four hours' climb up Kjerringdal. None
of them knew how far they had come, but there was
certainly a long way still to go. It was the sort of unwel-
come decision which nobody needs to discuss. With
hardly a word between them, they turned the sled
around and started back toward Mandal.

During the long weary hopeless journey back, the
blizzard did come on again in earnest, and proved the
decision was right. Going back, the wind was almost

behind them; they could never have made any progress going south against it.

When at last they got back to the steep edge of Mandal, they found they were some distance farther up the valley than the point they had started from. This was simply due to the difficulty of setting a course on the plateau, but it had some advantages. To climb straight down into the valley from where they were would avoid Kjerringdal, which was certain to avalanche at any minute. There was no point in going all the way back to the place where Jan had been lying when they found him.

The question arose again of what to do with Jan. Remembering the experience of being hauled up the mountain, he was still very reluctant to go down again. Apart from the pain of it, it would have been such a depressing step in the wrong direction. Besides, he could see that the Mandal men were dog tired. They had been at full stretch for something like sixteen hours, and for tired men to try to lower him down to the valley in the blizzard had obvious risks for them all. They themselves thought that if he could face another few days on the plateau, he would really be safer there. He decided to stay.

They found him another rock which would serve as a landmark, and dragged him to the foot of it. They untied him from the sled, and stowed their spare food beside him, and then they built a low wall of snow to shelter him from the wind. This was all they could do for him, and in fact it was all he wanted. When it was finished, and they had promised to come up again, they turned downhill for home, and all vanished into the mist of snow, and left him alone again. For all the day's journeying, he was about two miles nearer Sweden than when he started.

15

The Last Duty

He lay between the snow wall and the rock for nearly three weeks. In some ways it was better than the grave: he could see rather more of the sky, although he could not see around him beyond the wall; and there was enough room to move about so far as he was able. But in other ways it was worse: it was more exposed to the wind and weather, and it was much more affected by the change in temperature between night and day. In the grave, it had always been a bit below freezing point. In the open, whenever the sun broke through the clouds it melted his sleeping bag and the snow around him till he was soaked; and when the sun dipped down at night toward the north horizon, his blankets and clothes froze solid. But although this was extremely uncomfortable it never made him ill. In conditions which were more than enough to give a man pneumonia, he never even caught a cold, because there are no germs of such human diseases on the plateau.

He was well stocked with food when they left him there, and different parties of men came up from the valley every three or four days to keep him supplied. None of it struck him as very nice to eat, especially after it had been thawed and frozen several times, and he had nothing to cook with. But still, one can live without such refinements as cookery and he was grateful for it. There was dried fish, and cod liver oil, and

bread. It was a question whether the bread was worse
to eat when it was wet or when it was frozen. There
was also some powdered milk which had to be mixed
with water. It occupied him for long hours to melt the
snow between his hands so that it dripped into the cup
he had been given, and then to stir the powder into it.
Later on, when the thaw began in earnest, an icicle on
the rock beside him began to drip. At the full stretch
of his arm, he could just reach out to put the cup under
the drip, and then he would lie and watch it, counting
the slow drops as they fell, and waiting in suspense as
each one trembled glistening on the tip. Sometimes
when the cup had a little water in the bottom, the
drops splashed out and half of each one was lost. When
he was feeling weak, this seemed a disaster, and he
would swear feebly to himself in vexation. But in the
end he invented the idea of putting a lump of snow on
top of the cup, so that the drops fell through it without splashing. It took hours to fill the cup. The end
result, with the milk powder mixed in it cold, was a
horrible drink, but it helped to keep his strength up,
and he drank it as a duty.

Sometimes in those solitary days, between the
chores which always kept him busy, he still had the
strength of mind to laugh at the contrast between himself as he used to be and his present state of elemen-
tary existence. Looking back, his life before the war,
and even in the army, seemed prim and over fastidious.
There was a certain kind of humor in the thought that
he had once taken some pride in his appearance, chosen
ties as if they were important, pressed his trousers,
kept his hair cut, and even manicured his nails. Grub-
bing about in the snow for a crust of bread reminded
him of a time he had had to complain in an Oslo res-
taurant because there was a coffee stain on the table-
cloth, and of how apologetic the waiter had been when
he changed it for a clean one. It had seemed important;
in fact, it had been important to him as he was in
those days. If the man he had then been could have
seen the man he was now, the sight would have made
him sick. He had not washed or shaved or combed his

hair for weeks, or taken off his clothes. He had reached that stage of filth when one's clothes seem to be part of one's body, and he smelt. But, luckily, what had happened to him in the last few weeks had changed him, and he did not mind his dirt. It had changed him more fundamentally than merely by making him dirty and ill and emaciated and crippling his legs. It had changed him so that it was quite difficult for him to recognize the spark of life which still lingered inside that feeble disgusting body as himself. He knew already that if he lived through it all he would never be the same person again. He would have lost his feet, he supposed, but he would have grown in experience. He felt he would never dare to be impatient again, that he would always be placid and tolerant, and that none of the irritations of civilized life would have the power to annoy him anymore. Travel broadens the mind, he thought, and he laughed out loud because the plateau was so damnably silent.

When he fell into a doze during those days, he often dreamed of wolves. This was a fear he had been spared during his first week on the plateau, because nobody had told him there were wolves up there; but there are. They sometimes attack the reindeer herds, and the Lapps on skis fight running battles with them. They seldom, if ever, attack a man, even if he is alone; but nobody could say for certain whether they would attack a helpless man if they were hungry, as they often are in the time of the early spring. The Mandal men had taken the danger seriously enough to warn Jan about it and give him a stick to defend himself. Later, when they realized that a stick was no good because he had not enough strength to beat off a rabbit with it, they brought up brushwood and paraffin so that he could fire it if the wolves closed in on him. Of course he had a pistol; but it only had three rounds left in it, and he said he wanted to keep them for bigger game than wolves. Jan felt it was silly to be afraid of an animal, or even a pack of them, which had never actually been known to kill a man, so far as anyone could tell him. Yet the thought of it worked on his nerves. Until he was told of the wolves, he had only the inanimate forces of the plateau to contend with. He had relied on his solitude, feeling as safe from a sudden intrusion as he would in a house with the doors and windows locked. With all the dangers that surrounded him, at least he had not had to keep alert for any sudden crisis. But now, as he lay behind his wall of snow, unable to see what was happening on the snowfield around him, helplessly wrapped in his sleeping bag, he knew he might see the sharp teeth and the pointed muzzle at any moment within a yard of him, or feel the hot breath on his face when he was sleeping, or hear the baying and know they were watching him and waiting. This, more than anything, made him feel his loneliness.

In the comparatively roomy space behind the snow wall, he could wriggle one leg at a time out of the sleeping bag and look carefully at his feet, which he had never been able to do inside the grave. They were a very disgusting sight. His toes were still worse than anything else, but the whole of each foot was so bad that it was frostbitten right through from one side to the other between the Achilles tendon and the bone. All the way up to his knees there were patches of black and gray. He had quite given up thinking of ever being able to walk on them again. As soon as he got to a hospital, he supposed, somebody would put him straight on an operating table and cut off his feet without thinking twice about it. He was resigned to that, but he still very much wanted not to lose his legs. Apart from the problems of keeping himself alive, he had thought more about his legs than anything else, wondering whether there was anything he could do to help to save them. He had made up his mind some time before about one drastic course of action, but in the grave there had not been enough room to put it into effect. He was still under the impression, rightly or wrongly, that gangrene would go on spreading, unless one got rid of it, like dry rot in a house. The source of it all was his toes. They were not part of him any-more, although they were still attached to him, and it seemed only common sense that he would be better without them. There was nobody he could expect to help him; but now the time and the chance had come, and he made his preparations to cut off his toes himself.

He still had his pocketknife, and he still had some brandy. With the brandy as anesthetic, and the knife as a scalpel, lying curled up on his side in the snow with his leg drawn up so that he could reach it, he began carefully to dissect them one by one.

It would have been best to get it all over quickly, but apart from the pain and the sickening repulsion, it was difficult to cut them; more difficult than he had expected. He had to find the joints. His hands were rather clumsy and very weak, because there had been some frostbite in his fingers too, and the knife was not so sharp as it had been. He grimly persevered, and slowly succeeded. As each one was finally severed, he laid it on a small ledge of rock above him where he could not see it, because he no longer had strength to throw it far away. After each one he had to stop, to get over the nausea and dope himself with brandy. Someone had brought him some cod liver oil ointment, and he smeared a thick slab of it on each wound and tied it in place with a strip of blanket.

This grisly operation was spread out over nearly three days. At the end of it, there were nine toes on the ledge. The little toe on his left foot did not seem so bad as the others, so he kept it. When he had finished, he felt very much better in his mind. Of course, there was no immediate improvement in his legs, but it gave him some satisfaction to have done something which he hoped would help to save them; it was better to know that the rotten revolting things were gone and could not poison him anymore. It made him feel cleaner.

After it was all done, he went back with relief to the simple routine of his daily life: feeding himself, collecting ice water, mixing milk, trying to clean his pistol; once in a while, as seldom as he could, rolling a cigarette with infinite care and finding the box of matches which he kept inside his underclothes next to his skin; trying to put ointment on the sores on his back without getting too cold; sometimes treating himself to a sip of brandy; and always keeping on the watch for new attacks of frostbite. It was terribly difficult not to lie there listening, imagining the sound of skis or the distant snarl of wolves. Sometimes he stopped up his ears to keep out the ghastly silence, and sometimes he talked to himself so that there was something to listen to. When people did come from Mandal, shouting, "Hallo, gentleman," from far off, the sudden disturbance of the silence was a shock, and often it took him some time to find his voice to answer.

They paid him faithful visits all those weeks, toiling up the long climb every third or fourth night. When they came, they always brought fresh food, and usually some dry wood to make a fire to heat a drink for him; but lighting fires always made them uneasy in case the smoke or the light was seen. Whenever he heard them coming, he pulled himself together and tried to look as alive as he could, because he had a fear at the back of his mind that they might get depressed and give him up as a bad job and stop coming anymore. On their side, they felt they had to cheer him up, so that the meetings were usually happy, although the happiness was forced. Sometimes there was even something to laugh at, like the time when one man forgot the password. The story of how Jan had shot the Gestapo officer had got around, and he had the reputation in Mandal of being trigger conscious and a deadly shot. So when this man found that the words "Hallo, gentleman" had quite escaped his mind at the critical moment, he hurriedly dropped on his hands and knees and crawled up to Jan on his stomach, keeping well under cover till he was close enough to talk to him and make perfectly certain that there would not be any unfortunate misunderstanding.

On one of their visits, Jan asked them for something to read. What he really wanted was an English thriller or a French one, because during the last couple of years he had got more used to reading foreign languages than his own. But nobody knew of anything like that in Mandal, and the man he happened to ask could only offer him religious works in Norwegian. He declined that offer, but afterward the man remembered an annual edition of a weekly magazine which he could borrow. Jan thanked him, and the heavy volume was carried up the mountain. But as a matter of fact, Jan did not read very much of it. He never seemed to have time.

Somebody had the brilliant idea, when Jan had been up there for some time, of bringing up a roll of the kind of thick paper which is used for insulating buildings. They bent this over Jan in an arch, like a miniature Nissen hut, and covered it over with snow, and blocked up one end with a snow wall. It was just big enough for Jan to lie in, and it protected him quite well. In fact, it sometimes seemed warm inside. But it had its drawbacks; whenever it seemed to be going to get tolerably warm, the snow on top of it melted and dripped through on him mercilessly, and made him even wetter than before.

Sometimes his visitors came with high hopes, but more often the news they brought him from the valley was disappointing. On one night soon after they left him there, two men came up full of excitement to say that a Lapp had arrived in Kaafjord and promised to take him either that night or the next, and they waited all night to help Jan when he came. But the morning came without any sign of him. For the next three successive nights men came from the valley to wait with Jan for the Lapp's arrival, and to make sure he did not miss the place. They kept watch for him hour by hour; but no movement broke the skylines of the plateau. On the fourth day they heard that the Lapp had changed his mind because of a rumor that the Germans had sent out ski patrols on the frontier.

During the next few days this rumor was confirmed from a good many different sources. Recently, everyone had been so completely absorbed by the problems of Jan's health, and the weather, and the journey across the plateau, that they were well on the way to forgetting about the Germans. It was a long time since the garrison had come to Mandal, and that had been the last German move, so far as anyone knew, which had seemed at the time to be part of a deliberate search. The Mandal men had got used to the garrison and begun to despise it. But now it began to look as if the Germans were still on the hunt for Jan and even had a rough idea of where he was. When Jan was told about it, he reflected that the Germans had got a jump ahead of him for the first time in his flight. In the early days, when he was on the move, they had never done more than bark at his heels; but now, it seemed, they had thrown out a patrol line right on the part of the frontier which one day he would have to cross; and unless he crossed it within a few days, he would have to do it in daylight. If only he had been fit, both he and the Mandal men would have treated the patrol as a joke, because like all Norwegians they had a profound contempt, which may not have been justified, for the Germans' skill on skis. Even as things were, nobody except the Lapp was deterred by this extra danger. If they could only get to the frontier, they were sure they would get across somehow.

But soon after this rumor started, there was an extraordinary event on the plateau which really did make them take the danger of Germans more seriously. The most remarkable thing about life on the plateau had always been that nothing happened whatever. Day after day could pass without any event, even of the most trivial kind; and Jan discovered that most of the events which he seemed to remember were really things he had dreamed or imagined. His commonest dream or hallucination was that he heard someone coming. One day, when he was dozing, he heard voices approaching. It had often happened before; but this time, as they came near him, he realized that they were speaking German. He could not understand what they were saying, and they soon faded away again; and when he was fully awake, he thought no more of what seemed a slight variation of his old familiar dream. But the next night, when a party from Mandal came up to see him, they arrived in consternation, because there were two sets of ski tracks which passed thirty yards from the place where Jan was lying, and none of the Mandal men had made them.

It was one of those utterly mysterious things which start endless speculation. Up till then, they had always regarded the plateau as a sanctuary from the Germans, partly because they had never thought the Germans would venture to go up there, and partly because the job of looking for one man in all those hundreds of miles of snow was so hopeless that they had been sure that the Germans would not waste time in trying it. Nobody could imagine where the small party of men who had made the tracks could have come from, or where they had been going, or what they had meant to do. They were not from the Mandal garrison, because that was always kept under observation, and the place was more than a day's journey from any other German post. They could not have been part of a frontier patrol, because it was much too far from the frontier. Yet if they were searching for Jan, it seemed an incredible coincidence that they should have passed so near him, unless there were hundreds of patrols all over the plateau, or unless they had a very good idea of where he was. Besides, to search in that secretive way was un-German. If they did know where he was, they would know he could not be living up there unless Mandal was looking after him, and their reaction to that would certainly be to use threats and arrests in Mandal in the hope of finding someone who would give him away and save them losing face by having to scour the mountains.

They argued round and round the mystery for a long time on the plateau that night, with a new feeling of insecurity and apprehension. It had been pure luck that the Germans, whatever they were doing, had not seen Jan when they passed him. There had been a snowfall earlier in the day which had covered the trampled snow around his lair and all the old ski tracks which led up to it from Mandal. But if they came back again, they would find the new tracks and follow them straight to the spot. Altogether, it was alarming, and the

only comforting suggestion that anybody thought of
was that the tracks might possibly have been made by
German deserters trying to get to Sweden. Nobody ever
found out the truth of it. Those voices in the night
remained a vague menace in the background ever after.

When the Lapp lost courage and changed his
mind, it was only the first of a series of disappoint-
ments. Hopeful stories of reindeer sleds expected at any
moment kept coming in from Kaafjord and other valleys in the district; but every time the hope was doomed
to die. After a fortnight in which all their plans were
frustrated and came to nothing, the Mandal men got
desperate. Every time they went up to look at Jan they
found him a little weaker. He seemed to be dying by
very slow degrees. Besides that, the spring thaw was
beginning in earnest, and with every day the crossing
of the plateau and even the climb out of the valley
were getting more difficult. The snow was rotten and
sticky already on the southern slopes, and the next
week or two would see the last chance of a sled journey
before the following winter. During the thaw every year
the plateau becomes a bog, crisscrossed by swollen
streams, and nobody can cross it; and after the thaw,
when the snow is all gone, the only way to move a
helpless man would be to carry him, which would be
even slower and more laborious than dragging him
on a sled.

So they decided to make a final attempt to man-
haul the sled to Sweden while there was still time,
using a larger party which could work in relays. Accordingly, six men went up on the night of the ninth of
May, and dragged Jan out of the paper tent and
started off again to the southward. But this attempt
achieved nothing except to raise false hopes once
more. They had only covered a mile or two when
clouds came down so thickly that they could only
see a few feet ahead of them. They could not steer a
course in those conditions, so they turned around and
followed their own tracks back to where they had
started, and put Jan into the paper tent again.

After this failure, Jan really began to get despondent. He never lost faith in the Mandal men, and still believed they would get him to Sweden somehow if they went on trying long enough; but he began to doubt if it was worth it. Nobody had told him much about what was going on, but he could see for himself what an enormous effort Mandal and the surrounding district were making on his behalf. So many different men had come up from the valley by then that he had lost count of them, and he had some vague idea of the organization which must lie behind such frequent visits. As time went on, it seemed more and more fantastic that the German garrison could go on living down there in the valley, in the midst of all this hectic activity, and remain in happy ignorance of what was happening. Every new man who came up to help him meant a new family more or less involved in his affairs, so that the longer Mandal had to go on looking after him the more awful would be the disaster in the valley if the Germans did find out about it. Jan knew, and so did the Mandal men, the results of the uncontrolled anger of Germans when they found out that a whole community had deceived them. It had happened on the west coast, and villages had been systematically burned, all the men in them shipped to Germany and the women and children herded into concentration camps in Norway. There was no doubt this might happen to Mandal, now that so many people were involved, and Jan had to ask himself what the reward of running this risk would be. To save his life was the only objective. When he looked at it coolly, it seemed a very bad bargain. There was no patriotic motive in it anymore, no idea of saving a trained soldier to fight again; looking at his legs, and the wasted remains of what had once been such a healthy body, he did not think he would be any use as a soldier anymore. If he died, he thought it would be no loss to the army: he was a dead loss anyway. And it was not as if he were married, or even engaged. Nobody depended entirely on him for their happiness or livelihood. His father had another son and daughter: his brother Nils would be quite grown up by now: and even Bitten, his young sister whom he had

loved so much, must have learned, he supposed, to get
on without him, and perhaps would never depend on
him again as much as he had always imagined. He wondered whether they had all given him up for dead
already, and whether he would ever see them again
even if he did live on. As for his wartime friends of
the last two years in England, he knew they would all
have assumed he was dead if they knew where he was
at all.

This idea only came to him slowly, in the course
of about ten lonely days after the last abortive journey.
It took him a long time to come to a firm conclusion,
because by nature he had such a very strong instinct to
live. But inevitably the time came, in the end, when
he unwillingly saw one duty left before him. His own
life was not of any overriding value to anyone but
himself; and to himself, life only meant a few more
weeks of suffering and a hideous death, or at best, he
believed, a future as a more or less useless cripple. The
life of any one of his many helpers, healthy and perhaps
the focus and support of a family, outweighed it in the
balance. He saw quite clearly that he ought not to let
them run any more risks for him, and he knew there
was only one way he could possibly stop them. His
last duty was to die.

To decide to commit suicide when one's instinct
is utterly against it argues great strength of mind. Jan's
mind was still active and clear, but his decision had
come too late. By the time he reached it, his body was
too weak to carry it out. He still had his loaded pistol.
Lying alone in his sleeping bag among the wastes of
snow, he dragged it out of its holster and held it in his
hands. He had used it to save his life already, and he
meant to use it again to end it. Until the last week he
had always looked after it with the love he had always
had for fine mechanism, but lately he had begun to
neglect it, and it grieved him to find it was rusty. He
held it in the old familiar grip, to cock it for a final
shot, but it was stiff and his fingers were very weak. He
struggled feebly with the simple action he had been
trained to do in a fraction of a second, but it was not

the slightest use. He no longer had the strength in his hands to pull back against the spring. He felt a friend had failed him.

Afterward he tried to think of other ways of doing away with himself. If he could have gotten out of the sleeping bag and crawled away into the snow, he could have let the frost finish the work it had begun. But it was a long time then, over a week, since he had had enough strength to disentangle himself from the blankets or move his body more than an inch or two. He thought of his knife too, and tried its edge; but it had not been sharp when he cut off his toes, and now it was rustier and blunter, and the thought of trying to saw at his own throat or the arteries in his wrists was so horrible that his resolution wavered, and he feebly relaxed and tried to make up his mind anew.

It was absurd really. He felt he had made a fool of himself. He had struggled so long to preserve his own life that now he had not enough strength in his fingers to kill himself. If he had not felt ashamed, he would have laughed.

16

The Sands Run Out

When Jan came to this mental crisis, the men who came up to see him noticed the difference. Up to then, he had always seemed cheerful, and none of them knew what this appearance had sometimes cost him. But now there was no humor left in him, and he would hardly speak to them. In fact, up to then the occasional visits of strangers had been all he had had to look forward to, but now he was almost resentful when he heard "Hallo, gentleman," because it meant that he had to make an effort when he wanted to lie in peace. He did not tell them till later about the conclusion he had come to. It simply seemed to them that he had lost heart. They went down and told Herr Nordnes that he was dying at last.

It had never occurred to them, as it had to Jan, that what they were doing might not be worth the risk, and if he had died up there on the plateau, after all the effort they had put into trying to save him, they would have been very much disappointed and almost angry with him. But they were certainly right in their fears. The weeks of exposure had really worn him down to the point when his life might quietly end without any further warning. Only one course was left to them, since they never considered just letting him die in peace. They would have to carry him down to the valley again, and try to fatten him up and build up his strength till he was fit for another attempt on Sweden.

There were the Germans to think of. No house in the place was free of the risk of a sudden search. At night, by that time, there was no darkness left at all, and it would have been taking too much of a chance to have carried him all the way down to the inhabited part of the valley in broad daylight. But the valley extends for ten miles beyond the last of the houses, and all of it is more sheltered than the open plateau, and a few degrees warmer. Somebody remembered a cave right up at the head of the valley. There was a meeting in the schoolhouse, and it was agreed that the only hope of spinning out his life was to cut their losses, bring him down and install him in the cave, and begin all over again.

This was a hard decision for them all, and especially for Jan when they told him what they thought. It meant going back to the stage of the journey he had reached when he was first carried into the hut at Revdal nearly six weeks before. It meant that everything he had suffered since then had been wasted. And it also meant, above all, that before he could ever hope to reach Sweden he would have to go through the ordeal of being hauled up the mountain again.

However, he was too far gone to care, and the Mandal men assured him there was nothing else for it; so he let himself be pulled out of the paper tent and lashed yet again to the sled. Six men lowered him laboriously down to the bed of the valley, throwing away the height and the distance which the past weeks had so painfully won.

While this party was bringing him down, another was preparing the cave, by laying a bed of birch branches and grass inside it. When they got him there and pushed him inside and finally left him, he was in a state of luxury which he had not enjoyed since Marius's barn. They had taken him off the sled, and after its wooden slats the birch bed was wonderfully soft. He slowly got dry, for the first time in a month; and when his clothes had dried out he even began to get warm, a sensation which seemed an entirely novel experience; and when he was warm he fell at long last into a dreamless sleep.

He lay in the cave for four days, sleeping most of the time. When he did wake he lay staring at the roof which was only a couple of feet above his head, enjoying the gloom after the snow glare of the plateau. The roof was damp, and there were sometimes drips on it. He found them fascinating to watch and study. When one of them was just about to fall, he would draw a trail with his finger on the slimy rock so that the drop slid down it and fell clear of his body. When he rolled a cigarette he prepared for it by laying trails for all the ripening drops which he could see, so that he could be sure to have his smoke in peace. During those days, he discovered anew the pleasures of the very simplest things; the delight of sleep, the joy of anticipating eating, the unutterable luxury of yawning.

The mouth of the cave was often darkened as a visitor crawled in beside him to feed him with the best that Mandal could afford and to attend so far as possible to any wish that he expressed. The visitors sat and gossiped when he was awake, and left him alone when he was sleepy. One day, they brought him the news that one of the German soldiers in their garrison had run away to Sweden, which gave them all a quite disproportionate happiness. Every day, whoever had come to him talked about the Lapps, who were now arriving in great numbers in Kaafjord and the other neighboring valleys and were being coaxed and offered rewards by the local members of the organization in the hope that sooner or later one of them would make up his mind to help. But Jan had stopped pinning much faith in Lapps. The only plan he had was to sleep till he really felt he had slept enough. By then, he thought, he would be stronger, and that would be soon enough to think about the future. Then he would decide whether to go on leaning on the kindness of the Mandal folk still longer, right through the summer perhaps, or whether to put an end to it all as soon as his fingers could cock the pistol.

But suddenly, on his fourth or fifth day in the cave, a whole deputation arrived in excitement, to say that at last a Lapp had made a firm promise. He had demanded brandy, blankets, coffee and tobacco, which were all the most difficult and expensive things to get, but the organization was sure to be able to find enough to satisfy him, and people who knew him said he was a reliable character who would not change his mind. But his reindeer were still up on the plateau, and he did not want to bring them down and then have to take them up again. So to make sure of not missing the chance, Jan would have to be moved straight away and hauled up to the plateau to meet the Lapp and his herd.

Jan was not really ready to leave the comfortable cave. A little more rest would have made him fitter to start the struggle again. But he could not refuse to fall in with a plan which had raised the hopes of the Mandal men so high; and although he had been disappointed too often, it did seem that this might be the opportunity they had all been waiting for. He tried to show more enthusiasm than he felt, and they pulled him out into the glaring daylight and tied him down to the familiar slats of the sled again.

A large party of men assembled for the climb out of the valley. Eight actually took part in it. In many ways this ascent was less arduous, at least for Jan, than the earlier one from Revdal. There were twice as many men to handle the sled; and by then Jan was much less of a load to carry. His weight ultimately fell to 78 pounds, which was less than half what he weighed when he left the Shetland Islands.

The eight men were therefore able to carry him bodily for a lot of the way, and he was not so often left hanging feet downward or upside down. But the ascent lasted no less than thirteen hours, and by the time they got him to the top Jan was exhausted, and the good effect of his rest in the cave had been undone. After these hours of rough handling, he got angry for the first time in all those weeks, and in his weakness he forgot that he owed absolutely everything to the men who were carrying him. One of them had promised to bring tobacco for him, and in the excitement it had been forgotten. When Jan heard of this, it seemed for some reason the last straw. The prospect of even a day or two on the plateau without a cigarette was too much for him, and he snapped irritably, "You would go and forget the most important thing of the lot." It was an absurdly ungrateful thing to say, especially when tobacco was so rare and expensive that almost everyone in Mandal had had to give up smoking. But none of them took any notice, because they could see he had been pushed almost beyond endurance and was not really aware anymore of what he was saying.

As a matter of fact, the organization in Mandal and Kaafjord was being remarkably thoughtful and efficient, as it had been throughout the operation. When the climbing party got Jan to the new rendezvous on the plateau where he was to meet the Lapp, two men from Kaafjord had already arrived there. They had been detailed to relieve the climbers by taking over Jan and looking after him until the Lapp arrived, and they had been chosen as Lapp interpreters. The Lappish language is said to have no relation to any other language in the world except Hungarian, and there are very few people except the Lapps who understand it. Most of the Lapps themselves can also speak one or another of the languages of the countries they live in, either Swedish, Norwegian or Finnish, but the man who was expected that night was a Finnish Lapp, and so he and Jan would not have a single word in common.

The men who had brought him up were tired out when they got to the meeting place, so they handed Jan over to the Kaafjord men and retreated to the valley without any further delay. These two stayed with him to keep him company all through the following night. But events began to take a course which was terribly familiar. Jan lay passively on the sled while the chill of the night froze the dampness of the day in his clothes. The men who were guarding him watched the snow-bound horizon patiently hour by hour. But no sign of the Lapp was seen, and nothing stirred. In the early morning, the men had to go down to their

daily work, and Jan was abandoned again to his solitude.

The vigil began again with all its rigor and discomfort and the same hopeless dreariness. He was in a
different place on the plateau, but it looked almost exactly the same. There was no rock with icicles to fill
his cup, and there was no snow wall or paper tent. The
snow immediately around him was clean and fresh,
not stained and foul by weeks of improvised existence.
But the low hills and the dead shallow valleys within
his vision could hardly be distinguished from any others, and the familiar numbing cold, the snow glare and
the silence made the days in the cave appear like a
half-remembered dream which had done nothing but
give a fleeting glimpse of comfort and so emphasize
the misery of the plateau. He lay dazed, floating into
and out of coma, and he began to listen again. The thin
wind sighed on a distant hill, and stirred the loose
snow in feeble eddies with an infinitesimal rustle, and
died to silence again. In his moments of clarity he
knew these soft sibilant sounds threatened another blizzard. When his mind lost its grip on reality, he heard
the wolves again padding secretively around him. He
began once more to start into wakefulness when he
imagined voices or the hiss of skis.

The next night two more interpreters came to
stand by him. One speaks of night and day, but by
then the midnight sun was up. It was broad daylight
all the time, and night only meant that the shadows on
the plateau were longer and that when they lengthened
the air became more chill. Throughout this brilliant,
glaring, frosty night the men watched over him. But nobody came. Jan had made up his mind that the Lapp
would never come. The sun passed across the north
horizon and climbed again into the east. The men had
to give up waiting, and went away, and left him to face
another glaring day.

Four days and nights dragged by before they
broke it to him that this Lapp had also changed his
mind and made the excuse that he was ill. It was no
surprise. Jan knew it before they told him. This time,

nobody could think of any alternative. To take Jan down to the valley again in the quickly melting snow was a- final admission of defeat, because they could never get him up again over naked rock. Down in the valley, there was nothing they could do except feed him till the Germans found him and took them all. To leave him where he was only condemned him to a quicker, kinder death. It seemed to them all, and to Jan too, that they had reached the end. For the first time, they had no plans whatever for the future, no hopes to offer him, nothing to say which would encourage him. The only thing they could have done in mercy would have been to deny him the food which had served to spin out his existence, and to let him fade out as quickly as possible and in peace. Whatever they did, they knew it would not be long. It was useless even to promise to come to see him again. When they left him they gave him food, but they made him no promise. They expected to come again, twice; once to find his body and protect it from the birds and wolves, and again, when the snow was gone and the earth was thawed, to bury him.

When their voices had faded and the last of them had gone, Jan lay quite still. The doleful wind ruffled his hair and sifted a little snow across his face. His mind was at rest in the peace which sometimes follows the final acceptance of death.

17

Reindeer

When he opened his eyes there was a man standing looking at him.

Jan had never seen a Lapp before, except in pictures. The man stood there on skis, silent and perfectly motionless, leaning on his ski poles. He was very small. He had a lean swarthy face and narrow eyes with a slant. He was wearing a long tunic of dark blue embroidered with red and yellow, and leather leggings, and embroidered boots of hairy reindeer skin with turned-up pointed toes. He had a wide leather belt with two sheath knives hanging from it. He was wearing it loosely around his hips, not around his waist, so that he looked all body and no legs, like a gnome. Jan had not heard him coming. He was simply there.

They stared at each other for a long time before Jan could speak. His brain was slow to readjust itself, and his memory was muddled. Had someone told him this man was coming? Had he dreamed it was all over? Was this a dream? At last, with supreme inadequacy, he said, "Good morning." The Lapp did not move or answer, but he gave a grunt, and Jan dimly remembered then that he probably could not understand a word he said. He shut his eyes again because he was too tired to make any effort to think what to say or do.

He had an uneasy feeling that he ought to know

who the man was and where he had come from. There had been a lot of talk about Làpps coming to help him, he could remember that; but it had all been a long time ago, and it had all come to nothing in the end. They had given it up as a bad job. He could not think of any

sense or reason in a Lapp being there on the plateau all alone. He looked again to make sure if he had seen what he thought he had seen, and the man was still standing there just the same, with his ski poles tucked under his armpits and no expression whatever on his face.

Jan could not rest with the feeling whenever he shut his eyes that someone was silently staring at him. He could not even tell if the stare was friendly or hostile, if the extraordinary creature he had seen was wanting to help him or fingering the long knives at the belt. He wished he would go away. It seemed to him that the man stood there for hours and did not move or speak or change his curious stooped position. But then, without any sound the man had gone. Jan was relieved, and sank back into the daze which this sudden apparition had disturbed.

In fact, this was one of the Lapps whom the ski-runner from Kaafjord had gone to see on his journey a month before. He had just arrived with his herds and his tents and family in the mountains at the head of Kaafjord, and he must have been thinking over the message all that time. When he had first been asked, the whole matter was in the vague imponderable future. Now it was in the present, and the first thing he had done when he got to Kaafjord had been to find out where Jan was lying, and then to go himself to see whether the story was true. He did stand looking at Jan for three or four hours. He was making up his mind. As soon as he had done so, he went down into the valley and announced that he was going to the frontier. Immediately the gifts which had been prepared for the Lapps who had defaulted were pressed upon him; the blankets, coffee, brandy, and tobacco which had been bought here and there at enormous prices and carefully hoarded for this purpose.

The next thing that brought Jan to his senses was a sound of snorting and shuffling unlike anything he had ever heard before, hoarse shouts, and clanging of bells and a peculiar acrid animal smell, and when he opened his eyes the barren snowfield around him which had been empty for weeks was teeming with hundreds upon hundreds of reindeer milling around him in an unending horde, and he was lying flat on the ground among all their trampling feet. Then two Lapps were standing over him talking their strange incomprehensible tongue. They both bent down and picked him bodily up, talking all the time, but not to him. For a moment he could not imagine what they were going to do; but then he understood he was being moved from his own sled to a larger one. They muffled him up to his eyes in blankets and skins, and stowed packages and bundles on top of him and around him and lashed him and everything down with thongs of reindeer hide and sinew. There was a jerk, and the sled began to move.

This had all happened so fast that Jan was bewildered. A few minutes before he had been lying torpid and alone; now he was being dragged feet first at increasing speed in the middle of a wild tumult, and nobody had given him a word of explanation. He squinted along his body, and saw the hindquarters of a deer which was harnessed to the sled. A Lapp on skis was leading it. It was one of the bell deer of the herd, and as it snorted and pawed the snow and the sled got under way and the bell on its neck began a rhyth-

mic clang, the herd fell in behind it, five hundred strong, anxiously padding along in its wake. From the corner of his eye he could see a few dozen of the leaders, jostling for position. The mass of deer flowed on behind; it streamed out in a hurrying narrow column when the sled flew fast on the level snow, and when the sled was checked the herd surged around it and also halted. Sometimes in these involuntary halts Jan found himself looking up from where he lay on his back a foot above the ground at the ungainly heads and large mournful eyes and snuffling nostrils immediately above him. But when this happened, one or the other of the two Lapps appeared, urging on the draught deer which pulled the sled, and sometimes giving the sled a heave himself till the obstacle was passed and the rumble of hoofs began again, and the snow hiss beneath the runners.

All day the enormous mass of beasts swept on across the plateau, cutting a wide swath of trampled snow which hid the tracks of the sled which carried

Jan: the most strange and majestic escort ever offered
to a fugitive in war. Jan lay on the sled feeling that
events had got beyond him; but he was content to let
them take their course, because he had seen the position
of the sun and knew that at last, whatever happened,
next, he was on his way toward the south and toward
the border.

Some time in the evening they halted. The two
Lapps gave him some dried reindeer meat and some
reindeer milk to drink, and then he saw them pitching
a little tent made of skins. The reindeer were wandering aimlessly around and digging in the snow with their
forelegs to look for the moss on the rocks far down below. Jan was left lying on the sled. On the whole he
was glad of this, because the tent was certainly only
made for two; but when he was left alone among the
deer he still found them alarming. They came and
sniffed at him, most obviously wondering whether he
was fit to eat, and Jan, who knew very little about the
tastes of reindeer, was not sure if he was or not. If
ever he shut his eyes, hot breath and wet hairy muzzles
woke him.

After the Lapps had disappeared inside the tent,
a most peculiar noise began to come out of it: a monotonous kind of chant which rose to howls and died
away to moaning. When the first eerie shrieks rolled
out across the plateau Jan thought they must be fighting, and when one of them burst out of the tent after a
little while and staggered through the snow toward him
with the knives dangling at his belt, he thought an entirely unexpected death was in store for him. But the
Lapp stooped over him and a waft of his breath explained the whole fearsome interlude. The Lapps were
drunk, and they were singing. They had been getting
to work on the brandy which had been given to them
as a reward, and one had come reeling forth on his
short bow legs with no more evil intention than to offer
Jan a swig at the bottle. It came back to Jan then that
years before he had either read or been told about
Lappish singing. It is called yoicking. It is said to be a
kind of ballad which tells stories of heroic Lappish

deeds, but it is not in the least like the usual conception of music, and to people who have not been instructed in its arts it is apt to seem no more than a mournful wail, like a dog's howling at the moon, but somewhat sadder.

The day's sudden journey had revived Jan's interest in life, and when the Lapp thrust the brandy bottle at him he laughed: for a moment, with the wry humor which never left him except on the verge of death, he had had a glimpse of the ludicrous indignity, after all that had happened before, of being slaughtered by a drunken Lapp on the very last stage of the way to the frontier. He took a small sip from the bottle and was glad of it, but the Lapp began to talk. Not a single word he said conveyed anything to Jan, but the general meaning was clear enough. He was pressing Jan to drink more, with the embarrassing hospitality of drunk people of any nation, and he was going to be offended if Jan refused. But Jan knew from the experience of the last few weeks that one sip was enough to make him feel better, and that two might make him a great deal worse. So he smiled and shut his eyes and shammed unconscious, and after a while the Lapp finished the bottle himself and wandered back to the tent to start yoicking again.

It was a good thing to be relieved of the expectation of being murdered, but the situation was alarming still. As the lugubrious sounds of revelry rolled out again, Jan thought of the German voices he had heard in the night, and of the ski patrols which were said to be out on the frontier. He had no idea how far he was from the frontier, but the dreadful noise in the quiet frosty air sounded as if a patrol might hear it miles away. It made him nervous and there was no possible way he could hope to persuade them to stop it.

From time to time the Lapps made further sorties to offer him drinks or merely to look at him. Sometimes the bottles they brought were full, and sometimes nearly empty. He wondered how many bottles the organization had bought, and how long it would be before the two men got over this rare and splendid orgy and were fit to go on with the journey again. He was so helplessly in their hands. He felt as a passenger in an airplane might feel if he discovered the pilot and crew were very far from sober. All in all, he spent an anxious night.

But during the night the singing slowly flagged and gave place to a blessed silence, and some time in the morning the tent shook and the Lapps emerged, apparently none the worse, and immediately set about striking the tent and harnessing the reindeer. They seemed as brisk as ever. He thought they must have remarkable constitutions. Soon the herd was rounded up, the sled started, and the headlong rush of hoofs began again.

On this second day Jan lost the last of his sense of position and direction. He did not know where he was being taken, and he could not ask what plans the Lapps had made, or try to change them whatever they might be. But simply because there was something happening, some positive action going on at last, he had roused himself out of his mental apathy, and even felt physically better than he had when all hope had seemed to have come to an end. The lurching and swaying of the sled and its sudden stops and starts were sickening and tiring, but he summoned up every bit of strength which he still possessed, inspired if not by hope, at least by curiosity. He wanted to see what was going to happen next. This wish in itself must have helped him to keep alive.

Everything happened very quickly. The sled lurched to a halt, perhaps for the hundredth time. The herd, swept on by its own momentum, came milling all around him again. Then he found that both the Lapps were trying to tell him something. They were pointing with their ski poles. He tried to look in the direction they showed him but he could not see very much between the hundreds of legs of deer. He listened to what they were saying, but it meant nothing to him at all. And then he caught a single word, the first word they had ever said which he understood. It was "Kilpisjarvi," and he remembered it. It is the name of a lake. He looked again, with a sudden uncontrollable excitement, and caught a glimpse of a steep slope which fell away from where the herd was standing, and down below, at the foot of the slope, an enormous expanse of smooth unsullied snow. It was the frozen lake, in sight; and he had remembered that the frontier runs across the middle of it. The low banks of snow on the other side were Sweden. Slowly there dawned the wild incredible hope that he was going to win.

The Lapps were still talking. He shut his mind to that blinding blaze of hope, and tried to attend to them. They picked up handfuls of sodden snow and squeezed it so that the water ran down, pointed again to the lake and shook their heads. That was it: they were trying to tell him that the thaw had gone too far and the ice of the lake was rotten and unsafe. He looked down at the lake again, and then he saw here and there the greenish translucent patches which showed where the ice was melting.

He remembered Kilpisjarvi on the map. It was miles long, seven or eight at least, and the head of it was near the summer road, where there was sure to be a guard post. At the other end there must be a river. It came back to him: there was a river, and the frontier ran down it. But if the lake was melting, the river ice would surely be broken up and the river in spate and uncrossable. They must cross the lake: they must chance it: he had to make them try. Stop the herd, let him try it alone on the sled: one man on skis, one deer and the sled. But he could not explain it. He started to say it in Norwegian but their faces were blank and he stopped in an agony of frustration, and began again to try to control his impatience and to think of a way to make it all clear to them by dumb show. If only he had a pencil and paper to draw maps and pictures—

There was a crack, the unmistakable lash of a bullet overhead and then the report of a rifle. The deer froze where they stood and raised their heads, scenting danger. The Lapps froze, silent and staring. Jan struggled to raise his head. There were six skiers on the crest of another hill. One of them was kneeling with a rifle, and in the split second while Jan glanced at them another shot went over and he saw three of the men turn down off the crest and come fast toward the herd.

After seconds of stunned silence the Lapps started talking in shrill excited voices. Jan found he was shouting, "Get on, Get on! Across the lake!" The deer moved nervously, running together in groups, stopping to sniff the wind. The Lapps glanced at him and back at the patrol, the picture of indecision. The patrol was down off the hill, racing across the flats. In an access of frenzied strength Jan half raised his head and shoulders from the sled, forgetting that words were useless, shouting, "They're out of range! For God's sake move! Move!" One of the Lapps shouted back a quick meaningless answer. The other waved both hands toward the rifleman as if he was begging him not to shoot. In an inspiration Jan fumbled in his jacket and drew his useless automatic and brandished it at the Lapps. They stared at it aghast: heaven knows what they thought, whether Jan was meaning to threaten them or defend them. With a final glance at the skiers approaching, one jumped to the head of the deer which pulled the sled. The other shouted and suddenly, like a flood released, the herd poured over the edge of the hill and down the steep slope toward the lake, the sled rocking and careering down among them, snow flying from the pounding hoofs, rifle shots whining past and over, across the frozen beach, out in a mad stampede on to the slushy groaning ice and away full tilt toward the Swedish shore.

Epilogue

Escape stories end when freedom and safety are reached, but this story can hardly be ended without telling what happened to the people in it after it was all over.

Jan and Marius and the Mandal men had dreamed so long of the Swedish frontier that they had never thought much about what would happen on the other side of it. Of course they all knew it was a very long way from the border to a town or hospital, but to travel in a country where there were no Germans seemed so absurdly easy that none of them worried about the distance.

But as it turned out it was quite a long time after the hectic dash across the lake before Jan was put to bed in a Swedish hospital. Once the tension was over, his memory went to pieces. He remembers a day which he spent in a hut with a lot of Lapps, and another day in a canoe going down a fast river of which one bank was Finland and therefore controlled by the Germans, and the other Sweden. Eventually the river led to a telegraph station, where the operator sent an urgent message to the Swedish Red Cross.

That excellent organization sent an ambulance seaplane, which made a perilous landing on a stretch of the river where the ice was still breaking up. Before the plane could take off again, a squad of men had to break more of the ice to give it a longer run. The take-off was the last of the experiences which Jan recollects as having scared him out of his wits. After it, he had a

complete blank in his memory until a doctor told him
he had been in hospital for a week.

In hospital, he had the very unusual satisfaction
of being asked what surgeon had amputated his toes,
and of saying with a casual air that he had done it
himself; and later he had a satisfaction which was even
greater, when he was told that his operation had saved
his feet. The decision about his feet remained in the
balance for a long time. He very nearly lost them when
the doctors first unwrapped them; but they called in a
specialist who decided to try to redeem them, and
after three months' treatment they were declared to be
safe.

As soon as he woke up in hospital, he began to
try to get a confidential report of what had happened
through to London. It was not very easy. As Sweden
was neutral, there were naturally Germans and German agents around, and if his report had got into the
wrong hands, of course it would have been a death
warrant for the people in Norway who had helped
him. He was worried too by the recollection that the
Swedes had only let him out of prison three years before on condition that he left the country, so that they
had every right to put him in again. But some of his
story had filtered across the border, and no doubt the
Swedes who heard rumors of it felt he had earned the
best treatment they could give him. They let him get
into touch with a secretary in the Norwegian embassy,
and to her he dictated all that he could remember of the
story.

In England, we already knew, of course, that the
expedition had come to grief, and vague reports had
come through of what had happened to the *Brattholm*.
There had been a long, sarcastic and gloating story in
the *Deutsche Zeitung* about the brave and ever-vigilant
defenders who had won the battle of Toftefjord, and
this German view of the affair had even been quoted
in brief in the London papers in early June, while Jan
was still lying unconscious. But Jan's report gave the
first news of the unlucky chance which had betrayed the
landing, and it was also the first indication we had that

one of the twelve men who had sailed from Shetland
had survived.

Jan himself flew back to England in the autumn,
after being away from his unit for seven months. In
some ways, his return to wartime London must have
been a disappointment to him after he had dreamed of
it for so long. When the welcoming drinks and the official compliments were over, there was hardly anyone
he wanted to talk to about what had happened to
him. The Linge Company in which he had been trained
was a company of adventurers, and nobody in it talked
much about personal experience: for one thing, everybody in it was waiting his own call to go to Norway
and knew it was best not to be burdened with other
people's secrets. The few staff officers to whom Jan
could talk freely had already seen his report and were
busy with other plans, and anyhow were sated with
stories of desperate adventure. There was nobody who
could share the pictures which were still so vivid in his
own mind: pictures of the endless snow, the cold, the
glaring nights, the procession of faces of people who
had offered their lives for his and whose names he had
never known, the sound and smells of the northern
wastelands, the solitude and hopelessness and pain. In
the busy, gray autumnal streets of London, these things
began to seem like a private dream: a dream which was
overcast and darkened by anxiety, because he did
not know what had happened in those desolate valleys
after he got away, so that he was haunted, for the
whole of the rest of the war, by the thought that his
own life might have been bought at the cost of appalling
reprisals. To help himself to live with this burden of
worry, he threw all his energy into the routine of army
life, and into training himself to walk and run without
losing his balance, and getting himself fit again in
the hope that he would be allowed to go back to Norway.

But if nobody in England could share in Jan's
anxiety, it had its counterpart in arctic Norway. For
month after month, in Furuflaten, and Lyngseidet and
Mandal, Kaafjord and Tromsö and the islands, all the

people who had helped to save him went about their
daily business in the constant fear that something would
still be found out which would give them away to the
Germans. But time passed and nothing disastrous happened, and the fear very slowly faded; and in fact the
Germans never discovered anything, and nobody was
ever punished for Jan's escape. Furuflaten and Lyngseidet survived the war intact, but Mandal, on the other
side of the fjord, was the very last of the places which
the Germans destroyed in a futile "scorched earth"
policy when their retreat began. The people were driven
out and every house was burned to the ground. For
a long time the valley was deserted. But now, it has
spacious new houses and its people have returned. The
valley is still as remote as ever: it still had no road:
but its placid life has begun again, and Herr Nordnes
has a new generation of pupils in a new school, the
sons and daughters of the men who went up to the
plateau.

As I write, the midwife of Ringvassöy is still at
work; the same people live in the cottage in Toftefjord;
and old Bernhard Sörensen, who rowed Jan across the
sound among the searchlights, still thinks nothing of
getting his feet wet at 82. But his son Einar died some
years ago, and the two grandsons who made Jan tell
them a story are grown up and have gone to work in
town, so that Bjorneskar is a lonely place for the old
man and his wife.

The village of Furuflaten is very prosperous.
Marius has formed a partnership with three other local
men, one of whom is Alvin Larsen, who was with
him that awful night when they dragged the sled up
Revdal. They are building contractors, and they have
also put up a factory in the village, just by the place
where they hauled Jan across the road below the
schoolhouse. In the factory they make concrete blocks,
and a special kind of arctic prefabricated house, and,
most unexpectedly, ready-made trousers. The business
is growing: they are starting on jackets to match the
trousers, and there is no end to their plans.

Marius, I am glad to say, married Agnethe Lanes,

whom he treated so roughly on the night they climbed up to the plateau. They are bringing up a family in a new house they have built beside the log cabin where Jan stumbled in at the door. Marius is beginning to worry about his figure, but he still has his quiet irresistible chuckle, and I think he always will have.

As for Jan, he got his own way in the end and was sent over again to Norway as an agent, sailing once more from the base in the Shetland Islands. So it happened that he was on active service there when the capitulation came. In the midst of the national rejoicing and the hectic work of accepting the surrender of the Germans, he picked up the telephone and asked for his father's number, and heard at last that his family was safe and well. When he was free to go to Oslo to meet them, his schoolgirl sister, Bitten, for whom he had worried so long, astonished him by being twenty and having grown up very well, as he saw at a glance, without the benefit of his brotherly hand to guide her.

Jan is a married man now. His wife Evie is American. Jan and his father work together again, importing mathematical and surveying instruments from abroad. To meet Jan, absorbed in theodolites and his family affairs, in his house in the pinewoods in the outskirts of Oslo, you would never guess the story which he remembers. But you would see for yourself that it has a happy ending.

Appendix I

CHRONOLOGICAL TABLE

March	24	*Brattholm* sailed from Shetland.
	29	Landfall off Senja.
	30	The fight in Toftefjord.
	31	Jan in Ringvassöy at the midwife's house.
April	3	Reached Bjorneskar.
	4	Rowed across sound.
	5	To Kjosen by motorboat: through Lyngseidet at dawn.
	5	to 8. Lost in Lyngen Alps.
	8	Found Marius's farm at Furuflaten.
	12	Across Lyngenfjord to Revdal.
	12	to 25. In the hut at Revdal. Ascent of Revdal.
	25	to May 2. In the snow grave.
May	1	Marius and Agnethe climb the plateau.
	2	Mandal men arrive: first attempt on frontier.
	9	Second attempt on frontier.
	22	Carried down to cave in Mandal.
	26	Carried up to plateau again.
June	1	Crossed the Swedish border.

Appendix II

A German newspaper account of the "Brattholm"
incident taken from "Deutsche Zeitung,"
June 8th, 1943

FISHING BOAT WITH STRANGE CARGO

British sabotage group rendered harmless on Norwegian Coast

In the twilight of a spring evening a large seaworthy fishing boat steams slowly out of a little harbor in the Shetland Islands. In the light breeze which blows in from the sea, flutters the Norwegian military flag—it has only been hoisted as the ship left port. No security measures were to be neglected. Even before sailing, everything had been done to prevent unwanted people approaching the boat or her crew. After all, even in England it is not every day that a fishing boat is made ready for a trip to Norway. No wonder the greatest pains were taken to get the enterprise off to a good start.

Twelve men comprise the crew of this boat as it sails toward the east. Anyone who overheard them would soon be able to establish that all the men were talking Norwegian. A certain Sigurd Eskeland is leader of the expedition. He was born on a mountain range in Norway, but his parents died prematurely when he was young, and so he left his native country and made his way, as so many did at that time, to the United States. For years in America he fought starvation, tried

233

his luck here and there, until at last he found food and
shelter and the necessities of life on a farm. When war
broke out, unemployment threatened again. Then one
day he was urged to go to England to join the Norwegian legion. For two days he thought the matter over.
But time had helped him to make a decision. The spec-
ter of being without food hung over him again, and
moreover he was being accused again of being a for-
eigner. And so he reported himself to the recruiting
center. A little later, he arrived in England. There he
underwent his military training, and also attended a
sabotage school and was taught to be a paratrooper.
Months passed, months that were used in London and
in Scotland to forge plans—not for the daring invasion that was always being talked about, but merely
plans to decide where and how and when the Norwegian sabotage troops could be utilized. And now at
last such an enterprise was under way.

Four days passed. Three men stand on the upper
deck of the Norwegian boat and look eastward. Today
they are wearing—according to orders—civilian clothing. They are the three men of the sabotage party.
The real crew are no longer allowed to show themselves.
Once again, to the best of their knowledge, all precau-
tionary measures have been taken. I hope, said one of
the men, Harald, that behind this fog bank there lies
our coast. For it was about time. Engine trouble yester-
day had forced them to slow down.

They sail on to a small outlying island which is
only inhabited by a few fisher folk. This really ought
to be an ideal hideout. They hope it will be, for none
of them feel happy on their lame vessel any longer—
especially since a German reconnaissance plane con-
tinually swoops over the boat. In the faces of these
twelve men on the fishing boat *Brattholm* there is
consternation: have we been recognized? It is true the
Norwegian battle flag has now been hauled down, but
there is still the danger that the German is not quite
satisfied.

For all three members of the sabotage party one
thing is certain: as soon as they get ashore they will set

up their radio and send this report to London—that the German air reconnaissance and coastal guard are very strong indeed. There is no way of slipping in unobserved. Not even a chance for a cleverly disguised fishing boat—though God knows there are plenty of herring barrels on board to disguise her. All one has to do is to take them to bits, without any fear that salt water will pour over one's seaboots, or that twitching fish will wriggle and slither away. No, all that has to be done is to open these barrels and there are wonderful well-oiled machine guns. And it is the same with the fish boxes, only they contain hand grenades.

Now the coast looms up out of the fog. A small bay is selected as it has high rocks to protect it. Here the boat will probably be well concealed. Somewhat reassured by this, but none the less anxious and nervous, the sabotage party paddles ashore in a dinghy. It is a fair distance they have to cover. So they are glad when at last they touch land and jump out on to the beach. After long years they have Norwegian soil under their feet again!

They set off in a direction where they can see smoke. An old woman comes toward them—the first Norwegian in their own homeland! What greeting and reception will they get on this far-flung islet? They begin to ask her questions. They ask for someone who understands engines and can help them to repair the engine of their boat. But the woman will not help them. Next they meet a boy. Yes, he says, he will fetch his father who is a fisherman. They seldom see foreigners there, he says. Harald looks at Sigurd. But Sigurd behaves as if he has not heard what the boy said. He tries to do business with the fisherman. No, says he, he can give them no advice. In their short talk he has already summed up these intruders. What is the meaning of it all, Sigurd wonders.

They go on and on, like spurned beggars in a foreign land. Again and again they are told with a shrug that no help can be given. So the three offer first money, and then food which had been specially issued to them for bribery. But even that is useless.

Their task unaccomplished, they can only go back, grumbling and tired, to the hideout of their boat. Damn it, what is to be done now? Over here the boat is no further use to them. They must bury its valuable cargo. A thousand kilograms of dynamite are stowed in the hold. Where to put it? First of all let's get back, says Sigurd, to look at the maps on board and think it over! Little do they imagine what surprise awaits them.

Downcast by their cool reception in their one-time homeland, by the unsuccessful pleading and attempts at bribery, they push off again in their dinghy. Hardly have they come in sight of their boat when close by they see a German warship. They turn toward land again, there is yet one more chance—escape! But they hear the shout of "Halt!" The three of them row with all their might. A burst of machine-gun fire from the warship sweeps over the water. Onward! shouts Sigurd. A fresh wave of machine-gun bullets smashes the side of the boat. The water begins to rise in it. There is nothing for it but to swim for shore. And now they see that two boats have cast off from the German warship. They are trying to cut off their escape. It is a matter of life and death! The water is cold, it grips the heart.

When finally they get to land, a party of German soldiers and sailors is waiting to receive them. The long swim in the cold water, the strong current, and perhaps also their experience ashore, have taken more toll of their strength than they realized. Helpless, shivering with cold, with no will power left, they drag themselves up the stone quay—and give themselves up as prisoners. Sabotage operation "M" is broken up. Norwegians, who once believed they were helping to free their country, have once again been cynically and uselessly sacrificed by England. When their countrymen who had taken part in the capture heard the Wehrmacht communiqué, they expressed their verdict in a single word: "Misled."

BANTAM WAR BOOKS

Introducing a new series of carefully selected books that cover the full dramatic sweep of World War II heroism—viewed from all sides and in all branches of armed service, whether on land, sea or in the air. Most of the volumes are eye-witness accounts by men who fought in the conflict—true stories of brave men in action.

Each book in this series has a dramatic cover painting plus specially commissioned drawings, diagrams and maps to aid readers in a deeper understanding of the roles played by men and machines during the war.

FLY FOR YOUR LIFE by Larry Forrester

The glorious story of Robert Stanford Tuck, Britain's greatest air ace, credited with downing 29 enemy aircraft. Tuck was himself shot down 4 times and finally captured. However, he organized a fantastic escape that led him through Russia and back to England to marry the woman he loved.

THE FIRST AND THE LAST
by Adolf Galland

The top German air ace with over 70 kills, here is Galland's own story. He was commander of all fighter forces in the Luftwaffe, responsible only to Goëring and Hitler. A unique insight into the German side of the air war.

SAMURAI by Saburo Sakai with
Martin Gaidin & Fred Saito

The true account of the legendary Japanese combat pilot. In his elusive Zero, Sakai was responsible for downing 64 Allied planes during the war. SAMURAI is a powerful portrait of a warrior fighting for his own cause. (May)

BRAZEN CHARIOTS by Robert Crisp

The vivid, stirring, day-by-day account of tank warfare in the African desert. Crisp was a British major, who in a lightweight Honey tank led the British forces into battle against the legendary Rommel on the sands of Egypt. (June)

REACH FOR THE SKY by Paul Brickhill

The inspiring true story of Douglas Bader. The famous RAF fighter pilot who had lost both legs, Bader returned to the service in World War II as a combat pilot and downed 22 planes in the Battle of Britain. Shot down, Bader survived the war in a German prison camp. (July)

COMPANY COMMANDER
by Charles B. MacDonald

The infantry classic of World War II. Twenty-two-year-old MacDonald, a U.S. infantry captain, led his men in combat through some of the toughest fighting in the war both in France and Germany. This book tells what it is really like to lead men into battle. (September)

Bantam War Books are available now unless otherwise noted. They may be obtained wherever paperbacks are sold.

BOOKS BEHIND THE LINES:

The side of war you will never read about in history books

☐	2501	**THE HOUSE ON GARIBALDI STREET** Isser Harel	$1.95
☐	12492	**THE WAR AGAINST THE JEWS** Lucy S. Dawidowicz 1933-1945	$2.95
☐	2858	**THE UPSTAIRS ROOM** Johanna Reiss	$1.25
☐	11405	**THE HIDING PLACE** Corrie ten Boom	$1.95
☐	11407	**THE PAINTED BIRD** Jerzy Kosinski	$1.95
☐	10619	**FAREWELL TO MANZANAR** Jeanne Wakatsuki Houston and James D. Houston	$1.50
☐	12347	**SUMMER OF MY GERMAN SOLDIER** Bette Greene	$1.75
☐	12510	**THE LAST OF THE JUST** Andre Schwarz-Bart	$2.95
☐	10482	**90 MINUTES AT ENTEBBE** Dan Stevenson	$1.95
☐	12097	**HIROSHIMA** John Hersey	$1.95

Buy them at your local bookstore or use this handy coupon for ordering:

THE SECOND WORLD WAR

The full drama of World War II is captured in this new series of books about a world on fire. In addition to paintings, there are maps and line drawings throughout the text at points where they are most informative.

☐ 11642   **FLY FOR YOUR LIFE by Larry Forester**   **$1.95**
Amazing story of R.R. Stanford Tuck, one of Britain's foremost air aces.

☐ 11709   **THE FIRST AND THE LAST by Adolf Galland**   **$1.95**
Unique view of German air war by commander of all fighter forces in the Luftwaffe.

☐ 11035   **SAMURAI by Sakai with Caidin and Saito**   **$1.95**
Sakai's own story by the Japanese combat pilot responsible for shooting down 64 allied planes.

☐ 11812   **BRAZEN CHARIOTS by Robert Crisp**   **$1.95**
Vivid story of war, of fighting in tanks in the wide spaces of the Western Desert told by Major Robert Crisp.

These large format (8½ X 11), full-color art books capture the spirit of men and machines in action.

☐ 01063 **THE AVIATION ART OF KEITH FERRIS $7.95**
                                    Canada $8.95
☐ 01049 **THE AVIATION ART OF FRANK WOOTON $6.95**
☐ 01004 **THE MARINE PAINTINGS OF CARL EVERS $5.95**
☐ 01029 **THE MARINE PAINTINGS OF CHRIS MAYGAR $6.95**

Buy them at your local bookstore or use this handy coupon for ordering:

Bantam Books, Inc., Dept. WW, 414 East Golf Road, Des Plaines, Ill. 60016

Please send me the books I have checked above. I am enclosing $_____
(please add 50¢ to cover postage and handling). Send check or money order
—no cash or C.O.D.'s please.

Mr/Mrs/Miss_____

Address_____

City_____State/Zip_____

WW—6/78

Please allow four weeks for delivery. This offer expires 12/78.

Bantam Book Catalog

Here's your up-to-the-minute listing of over 1,400 titles by your favorite authors.

This illustrated, large format catalog gives a description of each title. For your convenience, it is divided into categories in fiction and non-fiction—gothics, science fiction, westerns, mysteries, cookbooks, mysticism and occult, biographies, history, family living, health, psychology, art.

So don't delay—take advantage of this special opportunity to increase your reading pleasure.

Just send us your name and address and 50¢ (to help defray postage and handling costs).